HOT TOPICS
IN THE
LEGAL PROFESSION
•
2017

Hot Topics
in the
Legal
Profession

•

2017

Benefit Tulane PILF Series

qp

Quid Pro Books

New Orleans, Louisiana

Hot Topics in the Legal Profession • 2017

The *Benefit Tulane PILF Series* of law books helps to fund the school's public interest organization and the placements it sponsors for the representation of indigent clients and public causes. More information is found in the Foreword.

Published in 2017 by Quid Pro Books.

ISBN 978-1-61027-381-7 (pbk.)
ISBN 978-1-61027-384-8 (hbk.)
ISBN 978-1-61027-383-1 (ePUB)

Quid Pro Books

Quid Pro, LLC
5860 Citrus Blvd., Suite D-101
New Orleans, Louisiana 70123
www.quidprobooks.com

Publisher's Cataloging-in-Publication

Childress, Steven Alan (ed.)

Hot Topics in the Legal Profession – 2017 / edited by Steven Alan Childress.

p. cm. — (Benefit Tulane PILF series)

Includes bibliographical note references and foreword.

"A timely collection of student studies on current events in legal ethics and the legal profession, discussing issues both important and changing during the decade of the 2010s."

1. Lawyers—United States. 2. Attorney and client—United States. 3. Practice of law—United States. 4. Practice of law—Asia. I. Title. II. Series.

KF 302.C29 2017

173' 12'7928—dc20
2017153482

qp

CONTENTS

FOREWORD

Ethics and the Legal Profession in a Decade of Continuing Change and Challenge

In the predecessor volumes, *Hot Topics in the Legal Profession 2012* and *Hot Topics in the Legal Profession 2010*, I offered the unsurprising observation that many issues of modern legal ethics and the structure of the legal profession move at lightning speed. Legal ethics and professional responsibility are not static mandates but rather use evolving concepts and rules. Beyond the legal ethics rules, bar opinions, and lawyer disciplines that have been at issue in the past five years, the entire legal industry, as with the economy surrounding it, has seen even more evolution and transition as of late. That is true both within the United States and in comparing the legal professions of other countries.

Ethics rules and bar discipline tell only part of the story of legal ethics. Beyond rules of conduct and their enforcement by bar organizations and judges, there is a whole world of law governing lawyers that is simply not about bar discipline or sanctions. Moreover, that is just the changing world of professional regulation, governance, and liability. The matter gets much bigger—and the changes even more pronounced—when one considers the legal profession in all its structural, economic, and social upheaval during this time: law firm layoffs and deferments, major partner moves and status changes, technological developments, compensation issues, the effect on legal education of reform proposals and fiscal reality (combined with mounting student debt), the shrinking of traditional law work and moving it in-house or abroad, and of course lawyer satisfaction and, in many situations, desperation. The professional picture expands even further when one ventures outside the United States and looks at changes the world over, in a time of economic instability, national debt and austerity reform, legal outsourcing, and corporatizing of law firms—or looks beyond the *legal* profession to other professions and industries such as medicine and finance. These stories and more dominated the headlines of the law media and bloggers over the past five years, and they promise to continue to signal massive and seismic adaptation to come.

All of this is to say that there is a lot of "law of lawyering" out there—and even more economic and social issues in the legal profession beyond rules of ethics as such. For each specific example, one could write a book. I have not done so. However, I have collected eight excellent essays from Tulane University law students that were written in 2017 about professional responsibility in law, as well as the legal profession more broadly, and I have edited them into this book on current events. We offer it not as a survey of the entirety of the field of ethics and the profession, but rather as a "selected topics" book, though one hopes it explores some of the most pressing and fascinating topics over the past few years.

The law students chose their topics independently, as part of the requirements to participate in an Advanced Legal Profession Seminar that we conducted in spring 2017. They performed independent research, discussed their topics with each other, shared editing ideas, and presented their unique findings in a formal presentation to the class (many using PowerPoint). I did not pick the topics for them, but I applaud their choices; they present some great topics, with current application and meaning, and I hope that lawyers, judges, and academics—as well as the general public interested in lawyers' roles and rules—will find them to be useful, as I have. Not every profound event in the profession is purported to be represented here, as it might in a comprehensive survey or yearbook, yet the topics explored here matter, and the students' research and views will prove interesting to a wide audience.

Anyone trying to keep up lately with the state of flux in legal ethics, and the profession writ large, will find some helpful tools in digital form, among them some daily-updated law blogs. In particular, the best sources for really current events in this field are *The Legal Profession Blog* and *Legal Ethics Forum*. Both blogs have been named to the *ABA Journal*'s "Top 100 Law Blogs" several times. And about these two blogs, *Capital Defense Weekly* once wrote: "[A]s someone who is petrified of effing up and losing the bar card, these sites are tops of my RSS feeds." Not to slight the other editors of these blogs (including myself, writing from time to time for *LPB*), but as to hot topics, I would say that the standout and prolific work of Michael Frisch (*LPB*) and John Steele (*LEF*), in particular, will keep any lawyer or bar observer current as to the state of the profession, rules changes, and discipline reports. There are other sources out there that help keep readers updated, too, including general purpose law blogs featuring occasional reports on ethics, the *ABA Journal*'s own blog, and the quarterly newsletters of the AALS Section on Professional Responsibility. Teachers, scholars, and practitioners in the field are lucky to have these resources on the legal profession and professional responsibility.

As to the selected topics in this volume, I commend to you their diversity of focus and depth of analysis. The timely topics include: conflicts of interest in corporations with subsidiaries and other related entities; technological changes to the profession wrought by automation and the emerging uses of artificial intelligence (AI); substance abuse among, and support programs for, law students and young lawyers, including an inside glimpse at lesser-known Adderall misuse; wrongful convictions and prosecutorial misconduct as an ethics matter; the new ABA model rule prohibiting discrimination, the problem of sexual harassment, and a comparison to earlier changes in the rules about sex with a client; and Rule 4.2's "no contact" rule and its application to self-representation in divorce cases. In addition, there are two essays on comparative and international perspectives by J.D. students from China, one analyzing employment issues for non-U.S. law students studying in the U.S. (both J.D. and LL.M. graduates), and the other exploring the development of the legal profession in China. All of these chapters are accessible to lawyers and also, since not bogged down with heavy legal jargon, to anyone interested in current topics of interest about the state of and conflicts in the legal profession and the justice system.

The student-authors of these chapters include current students who will graduate next spring (many of whom already write for and serve on one of Tulane's law journals or our moot court board), as well as a few writers who graduated after the seminar was completed and have since gone on to begin preparation for a bar exam. Those with legal experience in summer jobs and part-time employment—already having encountered the trenches of legal practice—certainly know by now how *real* the kinds of ethical and professional issues they explored in the seminar truly are, on a day-to-day basis. The course topics included problems of autonomy, confidentiality, cultural disparity, discrimination, and conflicts of interest that they surely recognize by now to be more than theoretical.

As much as I hope that readers learn from their product, as I did, I must stress that the students' primary purpose in writing these papers was academic. They supported our secondary goal of compiling this volume for public distribution, but I emphasized to them that their principal obligations were to the course and to their classmates. The result is that their papers were written, first, for that purpose, and with no pretense of turning this into a "law review" experience (though my editorial work was made easier, I am grateful to say, because so many of the students had writing or journal experience and were willing to share it with each other). I instructed them that they were to use a consistent and informative footnote style, but they were under no obligation to use a strict *Bluebook* format (indeed I told them to err on the side of more complete information or citations than they were required to give under the *Bluebook*). They were not asked to be sure that the style or formats they used were consistent among themselves (e.g., a reader may find variations not only in the footnote style but also in the textual presentations). Nor were they supposed to try to sound like a Spock-like neutral law review Comment; rather, I encouraged them to share opinions, make proposals, and even take stabs at tentative ideas. To the extent any contribution does not meet a reader's expectations about what typical law journal work by students should be, please blame me. This is not to suggest that the students do not succeed on such measures too; I could not possibly know, as the last time I saw a *Bluebook*, Al Gore had not yet invented the internet any more than Harvard law journal editors like Barack Obama and Neil Gorsuch had ciphered a way to cite it. I was focusing on the substance. The students certainly met my expectations, and those of their colleagues. So their important production, both in substance and in presentation, ought to be read by more than just our class internally. I am happy that, with the publication of this volume, it will be.

To that end, the students are not responsible for the reality of an inevitable lag time between their final drafts and the public publication. In most instances, the work remains as current as any such publication can be (short of immediate online blogging). And it is fair to describe this book as largely responsive to the current issues as of the summer of 2017. To the extent some current events may have superseded small parts of the analysis in this volume, again please blame me and not the students. I am confident that the students simply succeeded in the main purposes of this project.

There was another purpose as well. That is, this volume is the third work in the *Benefit Tulane PILF Series*, and its net proceeds benefit our school's organization, the Public Interest Law Foundation (which is not, I must add, responsible for any content or errors). Tulane PILF is a non-profit whose student members work tirelessly to promote legal representation of indigent clients and public interest causes, throughout the United States, by funding internships of students in law jobs for that purpose. PILF members, among other fundraising activities, run a fantastic and entertaining auction each spring; and they perform many other labor-intensive services throughout the year. All just to help their classmates have great public interest work experiences, and to help clients who need representation by the brilliant and eager young minds Tulane Law School can offer them. This book series, and the extra donations that may come from readers of PILF's web page, is offered in part to fund that need and remind people of the sacrifice and excitement for this cause that so many students at Tulane bring to bear when they volunteer for PILF. Whether the book succeeds on that level is entirely up to you.

Speaking for the student-authors of this book, thank you for purchasing it and considering their research, ideas, and opinions expressed in this volume.

STEVEN ALAN CHILDRESS
Conrad Meyer III Professor of Law
Tulane University

New Orleans, Louisiana
June, 2017

ABOUT THE AUTHORS

Steven Alan Childress is the Conrad Meyer III Professor of Law at Tulane University Law School, having taught there since 1988. He holds a law degree from Harvard and his M.A. and Ph.D. in Jurisprudence & Social Policy from Berkeley; he also clerked in the Fifth Circuit and practiced law in San Francisco. He is co-author of the appeals treatise *Federal Standards of Review* and a founding editor of The Legal Profession Blog.

Shu Chen graduated from Tulane Law School in May 2017, earning her J.D. She also graduated with a Master of Law degree in Admiralty from Tulane in 2015. Shu is from China and received her Bachelor of Law degree in Admiralty from Dalian Maritime University Law School.

Sarah Elizabeth Cullum is a J.D. candidate in Tulane Law School's class of 2018. She is the Senior Articles Editor, Volume 27, of the *Tulane Journal of Law and Sexuality*. She earned her B.A. in 2015, in English and Sociology, from Tulane University.

Marissa Delgado is from Long, Beach California. In 2015, she graduated from Cal Poly Pomona with her degree in Political Science and History. She currently attends Tulane Law School, class of 2018, and is a member of the *Journal of Technology and Intellectual Property* as well as an extern with the Louisiana Attorney Disciplinary Board.

Jessica Dennis graduated from University of Louisville with a dual degree in Psychology and Sociology, earning her B.A. in 2015. She is a member of the Tulane law class of 2018 and the Senior Managing Editor of Tulane's *Journal of Technology and Intellectual Property*, with a forthcoming Comment on smart contact lenses. In her third year, Jessica will participate in the Criminal Litigation Clinic.

Qinyu Fan is a member of the Tulane Law School J.D. class of 2018 and a member of the *Tulane Journal of International and Comparative Law*. In 2015, she earned her bachelor degree in Business Administration and bachelor degree in Law from the China University of Political Science and Law, in Beijing.

Corey Friedman was born and raised in Florida, where he attended the University of Central Florida in Orlando and graduated with a degree in Finance. Before attending Tulane Law School, where he is a member of the class of 2018, he was a data analyst for Lockheed Martin. Corey has also interned in the Middle District of Florida in the Bankruptcy Division.

Joshua Sanchez-Secor recently graduated from Tulane Law School in the class of 2017. While at Tulane, Josh was the Editor in Chief of the

Tulane Environmental Law Journal. He also graduated from the University of New Mexico in 2010 with a dual degree in English and Communication.

Vincent Yadgood is from Massachusetts, where he attended Northeastern University and graduated in 2014 with a degree in Political Science. Before attending Tulane Law School, in the J.D. class of 2018, he worked in the Massachusetts state legislature and interned with the U.S. House of Representatives. He participates in Tulane's moot court program as a coach and as a chairman for interschool competition.

HOT TOPICS
IN THE
LEGAL PROFESSION
●

2017

PART ONE

Application of Rules to New Settings and in New Ways

1

Duty of Loyalty or Limited Liability: How Close is Too Close for Lawyer Disqualification?

Joshua Sanchez-Secor

I. Introduction

Consider the following scenario: a law firm is asked to defend a lawsuit brought against an affiliated entity of one of the law firm's clients.[1] Is it a conflict of interest for the law firm to represent a lawsuit against the affiliated entity? The answer to that question is not obvious.[2] Moreover, determining whether there is a conflict of interest that would result in lawyer disqualification is a fact sensitive analysis with no clear guidance from case law or the American Bar Association's Model Rules of Professional Conduct. Two distinct areas of law intersect at the core of this issue: corporate limited liability structure and attorney's professional conduct. At this intersection, the question that necessarily arises is whether corporations receiving liability shields from affiliated entities can also disqualify its attorney's from representing lawsuits against its affiliated entities.

The issue raises a policy concern as to whether parent corporations should be allowed to benefit from corporate liability shields by claiming that it is separate from its affiliate, but also claim overlapping interests make the parent and the affiliated entity the same entity for disqualification purposes? Alternatively, should a parent corporation retain a liability shield by claiming that the parent's business is separate from their affiliated entity but then also receive benefits of an attorney's duty of loyalty and claim that it is the same entity as the affiliate for disqualification purposes? On one hand, if a law firm is receiving payments from a parent corporation's legal department, one may be inclined to say that the

---

[1] Kenneth Berman, "Litigation Ethics: Representing Corporations and Other Organizational Clients," American Bar Association Annual Meeting (Aug. 8, 2013), http://www.americanbar.org/content/dam/aba/administrative/litigation/materials/aba-annual-2013/written_materials/5_1_litigation_ethics.authcheckdam.pdf (last visited April 26, 2017) [hereinafter Berman, ABA Annual Meeting].

[2] *See id.* (citing ABA Formal Opinion No. 95-390 (1995)).

parent corporation is the lawyer's client. Thus, the attorney owes a duty of loyalty to the parent. On the other hand, should that same parent corporation claim that its lawyer cannot represent an action brought against one of the parent corporation's subsidiaries?

Hornbook corporate law explains that corporate veils protect parent corporations for exactly this reason—to distance the parent from the subsidiary for liability purposes.[3] Thus, it is seems fairly obvious why a corporation would claim that its subsidiary is unaffiliated with the parent corporation. Affirmative statements indicating separateness and increasing distance between the parent and any affiliated entity are necessary for defending against actions seeking to pierce the corporate veil. However, the corporation may jeopardize this position when seeking lawyer disqualification for actions brought against its corporate entities. Disqualification actions take the exact opposite stance and parent corporations essentially argue that it and its subsidiary are so substantially related and that the managerial controls between both entities substantially overlap, that a lawyer will breach their duty of loyalty to the parent if the lawyer represents an action against the subsidiary. Fundamentally, this seems like an unfair and opportunistic use of both corporate liability shields and lawyer ethical duties, with the corporation coming out a winner on both ends. This hypothetical scenario is the foundational and backdrop of this chapter.

Part II of this chapter introduces both corporate liability shields and lawyer ethical duties. Part II also addresses the model rules of professional conduct, specifically focusing on Rule 1.7. Rule 1.7 provides the framework for where the clash of corporate liability shields and lawyer ethical duties arise in corporate conflict of interest context. Part III of this chapter analyzes how the policy implications of corporate liability shields and lawyer ethical duties have created a wide array of opinions, but none of which directly address the policy considerations raised in this chapter. Part IV of this chapter directly addresses the policy question, which asks whether these two areas of law are really at odds with each other. Part V concludes this chapter, arguing that these two areas of law are not necessarily at odds with each other. Although at first glance it may appear that corporations are coming out as winners in both situations, disqualify-

---

3 RICHARD D. FREER, THE LAW OF CORPORATIONS IN A NUTSHELL 7 (7th ed. 2016).

ing conflicted attorney's preserves the policy goals of corporate structure and ethical representation.

II. Lawyer Ethical Duties and Corporate Liability Shields

A. *Lawyer Ethical Duties*

The story of whether litigating against a client's sister company violates the ABA's Model Rules of Professional Conduct begins with Model Rule 1.7. The rule states:

> (a) Except as provided in paragraph (b), a lawyer shall not represent a client if the representation involves a concurrent conflict of interest. A concurrent conflict of interest exists if:
>
> (1) the representation of one client will be directly adverse to another client; or
>
> (2) there is a significant risk that the representation of one or more clients will be materially limited by the lawyer's responsibilities to another client, a former client or a third person or by a personal interest of the lawyer.[4]

This rule, frequently referred to as the "direct adversity rule,"[5] protects clients from being represented by an attorney who also represents an interest adverse to the attorney's client. The policy behind the rule suggests that an attorney representing both sides of an action cannot sustain a level of confidence and trust from their clients.[6] Here, the rule seems fairly simple, essentially, an attorney cannot represent both sides of the same coin because representing both sides of the same coin may impair the attorney's ability to fulfill their duty of loyalty to each of their

---

[4] AMERICAN BAR ASS'N, MODEL RULES OF PROF'L CONDUCT, r. 1.7: Client-Lawyer Relationship Conflict of Interest: Current Clients (2015).

[5] RICHARD E. FLAMM, LAWYER DISQUALIFICATION: CONFLICTS OF INTERESTS AND OTHER BASES § 3.4, 47 (Banks and Jordan L. Pub. Co. 2003) [hereinafter FLAMM, LAWYER DISQUALIFICATION].

[6] *Id.*

clients.[7] So, when does Model Rule 1.7 become confusing? The confusion stems from Model Rule 1.7, comment 34, which states:

> A lawyer who represents a corporation or other organization does not, by virtue of that representation, necessarily represent any constituent or affiliated organization, such as a parent or subsidiary.... Thus, the lawyer for an organization is not barred from accepting representation adverse to an affiliate in an unrelated matter, unless the circumstances are such that the affiliate should also be considered a client of the lawyer, there is an understanding between the lawyer and the organizational client that the lawyer will avoid representation adverse to the client's affiliates, or the lawyer's obligations to either the organization client or the new client are likely to limit materially the lawyer's representation of the other client.[8]

Comment 34 introduces an explanation of situations that modern attorney's face. Specifically, when comment 34 states that "unless the circumstances are such that the affiliate should also be considered a client," comment 34 addresses situations where an attorney that represents a parent corporation should be disqualified from representing actions against the parent corporation's affiliated entities.[9] The issue for modern corporate attorneys is there is no clear guidance on where to draw the disqualification line.

As explained in a pamphlet provided at the 2013 ABA Annual Meeting in the Section of Litigation there are two different views on whether a conflict of interests exists when an attorney representing a parent corporation eventually represents an action against the parents affiliated entity.[10] Specifically, "[t]hose who see no conflict would argue that, as a basic fact of modern corporate life, a lawyer's knowledge of confidential information from [an affiliated entity] of a large corporate family is not information that could give the adversaries of an affiliate an advantage...."[11] Those who see a conflict of interest, necessarily take the

---

7 *See id.*

8 AMERICAN BAR ASS'N, MODEL RULES OF PROF'L CONDUCT, r. 1.7: Client-Lawyer Relationship Conflict of Interest: Current Clients, Comment 34 (2015).

9 *See id.*

10 *See* Berman, ABA Annual Meeting, *supra* note 1; *see also* AMERICAN BAR ASS'N MODEL RULES OF PROF'L CONDUCT, R. 1.7: Client-Lawyer Relationship Conflict of Interest: Current Clients (2015).

11 Berman, ABA Annual Meeting, *supra* note 1.

position that disqualification is appropriate when a lawyer's representation against an affiliated entity will be materially limited because of the duties that the lawyer owes to the parent corporation. Most importantly, courts are split on "whether a traditional client's corporate affiliate should be treated as a de facto client of challenged counsel for purposes of applying the conflict of interest rules."[12] Rather than treat the affiliated entity with a blanket prohibition, resulting in disqualification of counsel, many courts have created "a balancing test to determine whether disqualification is an appropriate remedy. . . ."[13]

Consider this imagined example of the type of scenario that comment 34 contemplates. PepsiCo Inc., a company incorporated under the laws of North Carolina is a parent corporation with 869 affiliated entities.[14] For the purposes of this hypothetical, assume that PepsiCo has a centralized legal department that retains a law firm to represent PepsiCo in a trademark infringement action. Next, that law firm is retained by a company specializing in social media advertising to advice on a contract the company is entering into with one of PepsiCo's 869 affiliated entities.

Eventually, after the advertising deal goes sour, the law firm is retained to litigate the breach of contract issue against one of PepsiCo's affiliated entities. By virtue of the law firm representing PepsiCo in the trademark infringement action, can the law firm be disqualified from the unrelated breach of contract issue? To illustrate the policy consideration this chapter addresses, those who argue that there is no conflict of interest argue that "[c]orporations that choose to do business as separate entities . . . ought not to be able to get the benefits of separateness without also accepting the burdens of separateness."[15] To put this argument in the context of the hypothetical, those arguing that there is no conflict of interest argue that PepsiCo has decided to operate as separate entities and cannot claim conflict of interest in the breach of contract action because PepsiCo has already stated that it is a completely separate entity. Here, it is important to understand why corporations choose to do business as

---

[12] *See* FLAMM, LAWYER DISQUALIFICATION, *supra* note 5, at 251.

[13] *See id.*

[14] According to the trademarked Lexis Corporate Affiliations search filter, 869 entities are organized under the parent corporation PepsiCo Inc.

[15] Berman, ABA Annual Meeting *supra* note 1; *see also* AMERICAN BAR ASS'N, MODEL RULES OF PROF'L CONDUCT, r. 1.7: Client-Lawyer Relationship Conflict of Interest: Current Clients (2015).

separate entities and why those who see no conflict of interest in the PepsiCo hypothetical want corporations to live with their decisions to do business utilizing separate entities, and prevent the corporation from disqualifying attorneys from unrelated actions against affiliated entities.

B. Discarding the Corporate Structure

Companies may choose to do business as separate entities to limit liability.[16] Normally, a company may choose to incorporate in order to protect the individual members of the company from liability.[17] This ability stems from a policy decision not to hold owners of corporations personally liable for the actions of the corporation. In order for individuals to limit their liability, they may choose to incorporate under state law and the individual members will not be liable for the corporation's actions.[18] To hold an individual member liable for the corporation's actions, a plaintiff must pierce the corporate veil.[19] This basic idea becomes more complex when corporations become shareholders in other corporations, and rather than simply piercing the corporate veil, courts discard the corporate structure.[20]

Discarding the corporate structure refers to a form of veil piercing, where courts disregard the parent-subsidiary relationship—which would limit the parent corporations liability for the subsidiary's action—and hold the parent corporation liable for their subsidiaries' actions. Because corporate law is regulated by state law, there are various factors that courts consider when disregarding the corporate structure and piercing the corporate veil. This is also known as an alter ego test,[21] or an

---

[16] *See* 1 FLETCHER CYCLOPEDIA OF THE LAW OF CORPORATIONS § 14 (Sept. 2016 Update) [hereinafter FLETCHER CYC. CORP.].

[17] *Id.*, §§ 41-48.

[18] *Id.*

[19] *Id.*

[20] EDWARD BRODSKY AND M. PATRICIA ADAMSKI, LAW OF CORPORATE OFFICERS & DIRECTORS: RIGHTS, DUTIES, & LIABILITIES § 20:15 (Oct. 2016 Update) (citing U.S. v. Jon-T Chemicals, Inc., 768 F.2d 686, 691 (5th Cir. 1985)) [hereinafter LAW OF CORP. OFFS. & DIRS.]

[21] *Id.*

instrumentality rule.[22] Generally, under an alter ego test, courts will consider "whether the parent's domination over the subsidiary was total and complete [or] whether the subsidiary was adequately capitalized" when determining whether to disregard the corporate structure and pierce the corporate veil.[23]

Whether the parent's dominion over the subsidiary was total and complete is not an easy question to answer.[24] For example, consider whether a wholly-owned subsidiary is completely controlled by its corporate parent by simply being wholly-owned. All shares of a wholly-owned subsidiary are owned by the parent corporation[25] and wholly-owned subsidiaries, generally, have many of the same directors and officers as the parent.[26] Many courts would likely hold that a wholly-owned subsidiary is not an alter ego of the parent corporation by simply being a wholly-owned subsidiary.[27] Rather, the inquiry is much more demanding, and control over the subsidiary must be a level of control that essentially prevents the subsidiary from thinking or behaving independently.[28]

---

[22] *See, e.g.*, U.S. v. Jon-T Chemicals, Inc., 768 F.2d 686, 691 (5th Cir. 1985) (citing 1 FLETCHER CYC. CORP. § 43 204-05 (rev. perm. ed. 1963) ("The control necessary to invoke what is sometimes called the 'instrumentality rule' is not mere majority or complete stock control but such domination of finances, policies and practices that the controlled corporation has, so to speak, no separate mind, will or existence of its own and is but a business conduit for its principal.")).

[23] LAW OF CORP. OFFS. & DIRS., *supra* note 20, § 20:15.

[24] *Id.*, § 20:15 (citing Devlin v. WSI Corp., 833 F. Supp. 69, 74 (D. Mass. 1993) (pervasive manner of domination may require treating subsidiary as agent of parent corporation)).

[25] *See* 16 AM. JUR. PROOF OF FACTS 2d 679 § 3 (Feb. 2017 Update); *see also* LAW OF CORP. OFFS. & DIRS., *supra* note 20, § 20:15.

[26] *See* LAW OF CORP. OFFS. & DIRS., *supra* note 20, § 20:15.

[27] *See, e.g.*, Intellectual Ventures I LLC v. Toshiba Corp., 66 F. Supp. 3d 495, 498 (D. Del. 2014) ("Simply being a wholly-owned subsidiary of a parent corporation alone does not make the subsidiary the agent of its parent; rather, [a] parent corporation will be held liable for the activities of the subsidiary only if the parent dominates those activities.") (internal quotations omitted).

[28] 16 AM. JUR. PROOF OF FACTS 2d 679, *supra* note 25, § 3 (Feb. 2017 Update) (citing Lowendahl v. Baltimore & O. R. Co., 6 N.E.2d 56 (1936) ("[I]t has been said that control through mere ownership of a majority, or even of all, of the capital stock, and the use of the power incident thereto to elect officers and directors, will not necessarily in and of itself result in liability of the parent, but liability must depend upon a dominion and control so complete that the subsidiary corporation may be said to have no will, mind, or existence of its own, and to be operated as a mere department of the business of the stockholder.")).

Consider *Phoenix Canada Oil Co. v. Texaco, Inc.*, where plaintiffs alleged that Texaco Inc. was liable for contracts breached by its subsidiaries.[29] The plaintiffs specifically alleged that Texaco Inc.'s subsidiaries were agents of the parent corporation.[30] To determine whether Texaco Inc.'s subsidiaries were agents of the parent corporation, the court considered factors such as: (1) whether the responsibility for the day-to-day operations was under the control of the parent; (2) whether the parent was responsible for the origin of the subsidiary's business and assets; (3) whether there was an overlap of officers and directors between the parent and the subsidiary; (4) how the subsidiary was financed; and (5) whether the parent was responsible for human resources duties.[31]

When considering these factors, the court discovered that Texaco Inc. and its subsidiary shared some officers and directors.[32] The court also discovered that the subsidiary could not make major financial decisions without the Texaco Inc.'s approval.[33] However, the court also discovered that the subsidiary was in charge of the day-to-day managerial operations in a foreign country, and that the subsidiary also carried its own books and paid its own taxes.[34] For these reasons, the court concluded that the subsidiary was not an agent of the Texaco Inc., and Texaco Inc. was not be held liable for contracts breached by its subsidiary.[35]

It is fairly common to demonstrate separateness through a variety of factors, however there are some occasions where the parent corporation simply does not do enough to demonstrate separateness. For example, in *Intellectual Ventures I L.L.C. v. Toshiba Corp.*, plaintiffs sought to hold Toshiba Corp., and other affiliated entities, jointly liable for patent infringement carried out by one of Toshiba Corp.'s subsidiaries.[36] Specifically, the plaintiffs alleged that Toshiba Corp. had instructed

---

[29] Phoenix Canada Oil Co. v. Texaco, Inc., 658 F. Supp. 1061, 1085 (D. Del. 1987), *aff'd*, 842 F.2d 1466 (3d Cir. 1988).

[30] *Id.*

[31] *Id.*

[32] *Id.*

[33] *Id.*

[34] *Id.*

[35] *Id.*

[36] Intellectual Ventures I L.L.C. v. Toshiba Corp., 66 F. Supp. 3d 495, 498 (D. Del. 2014).

one of its subsidiaries "to carry out the infringement of [the plaintiff's] patents."[37] The action was brought in Delaware where Toshiba Corp. was incorporated, and under Delaware law, "[a] parent corporation that directs the allegedly infringing activity of a subsidiary can be liable for its subsidiary's infringement."[38] This claim was addressed in a motion to dismiss the plaintiff's joint liability claim.[39] Therefore, it was Toshiba Corp.'s burden to demonstrate a lack of authority over their subsidiary.[40] However, Toshiba Corp. did not state any facts that demonstrated separateness. Because Toshiba Corp. did not provide facts demonstrating separateness the court denied its motion to dismiss.[41]

In both *Phoenix Canada Oil Co. v. Texaco, Inc.,* and *Intellectual Ventures I L.L.C. v. Toshiba Corp.,* the court considered overlapping managerial factors when determining whether the parent corporation could be liable for the acts of its subsidiaries. However, in neither example did the court consider whether a central legal department located within the parent corporation would direct the courts to find a lack of separateness between the parent and the subsidiary. This creates an interesting nuance when addressing the duty of loyalty that lawyers owe to their corporate clients.

In proceedings where courts look to discard the corporate structure, courts do not seem concerned about a central legal department that services the parent corporation and the parent's affiliated entities. Thus, the question becomes, if courts are not concerned about a centralized legal department when determining whether to discard the corporate structure, then are corporations really benefiting from both business organization law and the law regulating lawyers? If answered in the negative, then it seems that both corporate structure and lawyer ethical duties are not exactly and odds they can coexist. Before reaching that conclusion it is important to consider a few cases that address when it is appropriate to disqualify an attorney for representing an interest adverse to the parent corporation's subsidiary.

---

37 *Id.*

38 *Id.*

39 *Id.*

40 *Id.*

41 *Id.* at 499.

III. Lawyer's Duty of Loyalty Owed to Corporate Clients

Because a lawyer that represents a parent corporation may not necessarily represent an affiliated entity, courts have reached varying conclusions on when disqualification is appropriate. To make that determination courts generally focus on (i) the degree of operational commonality between affiliated entities and (ii) the extent to which one depends financially on the other.[42] Under the New York Rules of Professional Conduct, courts will consider, "(i) whether the affiliate has imparted confidential information to the lawyer in furtherance of the representation, (ii) whether the affiliated entities share a legal department and general counsel, and (iii) other factors relating to the legitimate expectations of the client as to whether the lawyers also represents the affiliate."[43]

In *Giambrone v. Meritplan*, the United States Federal District for the Eastern District of New York considered whether an individual attorney, who represented two entities under one corporate umbrella, should be disqualified from an unrelated action against the parent corporation's affiliated entity.[44] The court explained that the "core inquiry in determining whether affiliated entities should be considered 'clients' of an attorney is, considering the risks against which the ethics rules are designed to guard, whether those risks are actually present in this factual circumstance."[45] The court further explained that the rules were designed to protect against the risk of using client confidences against the client when representing it in the current action.[46]

The facts of *Giambrone* are complicated because of the defendant's role in the larger corporate structure. The defendant in *Giambrone* was an insurance underwriting company tiled Meritplan Ins. Co.[47] The owner of the Meritplan policies was essentially a parent corporation titled QBE Insurance Group and QBE Subsidiaries.[48] Additionally, two other QBE affiliates, titled QBEAI and QBE First, "assumed responsibilities and

---

[42] Giambrone v. Meritplan Ins. Co., 117 F. Supp. 3d 259, 269-70 (E.D.N.Y. 2015).

[43] *Id.* at 270.

[44] *Id.* at 268-71.

[45] *Id.*

[46] *Id.*

[47] *Id.* at 262.

[48] *Id.*

complete oversight for claims management and administration, adjusting, coverage and litigation management for Meritplan [insurance] policies."[49] The disqualification action addressed whether an attorney who formerly represented a parent corporation should be disqualified from representing an action against one of the parent corporations affiliated entities after lateraling into the new firm.[50]

The attorney previously represented QBE Insurance Group, but not Meritplan, in a variety of insurance matters from 2010 to 2013.[51] In March of 2013 the attorney lateraled to a new firm and eventually began representing plaintiffs Giambrone in the action against Meritplan. Meritplan argued that by virtue of working on a variety of insurance matters for QBE, the attorney had access to confidential QBE information, practices and protocol.[52] This argument was important because Meritplan attempted to show that there was significant institutional overlap between Meritplan and the parent corporation OBE. However, Meritplan failed to demonstrate that the attorney directly represented Meritplan at all, instead arguing that the attorney's previous representation of the parent corporation QBE created enough of a conflict of interest that warranted disqualification.[53] The court was not persuaded by the slight institutional overlap that Meritplan demonstrated.[54]

When dismissing Meritplan's argument, the court began by addressing the disqualification rules and when they should apply. Specifically, the court distinguished between concurrent conflicts of interest and successive conflicts of interest.[55] Next, the court explained that whether a conflict of interest existed depended on three questions:

---

[49] *Id.* at 263.

[50] *Id.* at 268.

[51] *Id.* at 264.

[52] *Id.*

[53] *Id.* at 265.

[54] *Id.* at 270.

[55] *Id.* A successive conflict of interest arises when an attorney takes an adverse position to a former client, whereas a concurrent conflict of interest arises when an attorney takes a position directly adverse to a current client. Model Rule 1.7 addresses concurrent conflicts of interest. *See* AMERICAN BAR ASS'N, MODEL RULES OF PROF'L CONDUCT, r. 1.7: Client-Lawyer Relationship Conflict of Interest: Current Clients, Comment 34 (2015).

> [Whether] (1) the moving party is a former client of the adverse party's counsel; (2) there is a substantial relationship between the subject matter of the counsel's prior representation of the moving party and the issues in the present lawsuit; and (3) the attorney whose disqualification is sought had access to, or was likely to have had access to, relevant privileged information in the course of his prior representation of the client.[56]

More importantly, the court also explained that the test is designed to prevent attorneys from acquiring confidential information while representing a client, then using that confidential information against the client in a future proceeding.[57] The court also explained that comment 34 to Rule 1.7 states that "representation adverse to a client's affiliate can, in certain circumstances, conflict with the lawyer's duty of loyalty owed to a client. . . ."[58] Thus, Meritplan's argument turned on whether the overlap between Meritplan and the parent corporation QBE was so substantially overlapping that they should be considered one entity for conflict of interest purposes.[59] Essentially, Meritplan argued that the attorney, through previous representation of the parent corporation QBE, had acquired confidential information that would be used against it during this particular action.

To support this argument, Meritplan identified a number of overlapping institutional factors. First, Meritplan argued that the parent corporation acted as its "accounting, audit, cash management, employee benefits, finance, human resource, information technology, insurance, payroll, and travels service and system for [its] property and casualty insurance businesses."[60] This part of the argument was successful in demonstrating that significant operational overlap existed because precedent had established that overlapping institutional factors include sharing corporate headquarters, payroll systems and a human resource departments.[61] However, the court maintained that "[t]he core inquiry in determining whether affiliated entities should be considered "clients" of

---

[56] *Giambrone*, 117 F. Supp. 3d at 268.

[57] *See id.* at 270.

[58] *Id.* at 268.

[59] *Id.* at 270.

[60] *Id.*

[61] *Id.* (citing HLP Properties, LLC v. Consol. Edison Co. of N.Y., No. 14 CIV. 01383 LGS, 2014 WL 5285926 (S.D.N.Y. Oct. 16, 2014)).

an attorney is, considering the risks against which the ethics rules are designed to guard, whether those risks are actually present in this factual circumstance."[62] As previously mentioned, Meritplan never demonstrated that the attorney ever represented it at any time. Without any fact demonstrating that the attorney possessed confidential information about Meritplan, the court determined that the relationship between the attorney and Meritplan was too attenuated, therefore disqualification was improper.[63]

The court in *Giambrone* seemed particularly focused on whether the attorney actually possessed confidential information, rather than focusing on whether the parent corporation and affiliated entity should be considered one entity for conflict of interest purposes.[64] It seems plausible that the court focused on the former inquiry partly because QBE, as the parent corporation, organized a very confusing corporate structure. It is not a stretch to read the court's reasoning this way because at one point the court addressed another QBE affiliated entity that may have been represented by the attorney, but neither party explained what that affiliation was.[65]

A simpler corporate structure was at the forefront of a similar case that the Court in *Giambrone* relied upon. In *GSI Commerce Sol., Inc. v. BabyCenter, L.L.C.*, the United States Court of Appeals for the Second Circuit addressed whether a firm that had entered into an engagement agreement with Johnson and Johnson (J&J) and J&J affiliates should be disqualified from an action the firm brought against one of J&J's wholly-owned subsidiaries.[66] In 2004, the law firm Blank Rome entered into an engagement agreement with J&J to represent J&J and J&J affiliates.[67] In the agreement, Blank Rome sought a waiver of any potential conflict of interest arising out of Blank Rome's concurrent representation of another

---

[62] *Id.* (citing Glueck v. Jonathan Logan, Inc., 653 F.2d 746, 749 (2d Cir. 1981)).

[63] *Id.* at 270.

[64] *Id.*

[65] *Id.* at 264 (explaining that an affiliated entity named QBE specialty may have been represented by the QBE attorney, but neither party explained how that entity was affiliated with the parent corporation or Meritplan).

[66] 618 F.3d 204, 206 (2d Cir. 2010).

[67] *Id.*

client.[68] In 2005 Blank Rome sent a letter to J&J seeking to amend the agreement.[69] In the letter, Blank Rome specifically stated that "[t]he Addendum to our current engagement letter stipulates that we represent only [J&J], and not its affiliates, subsidiaries, partners, divisions and joint [ventures]."[70] This agreement was the agreement that J&J would rely upon when moving to disqualify Blank Rome. The court also noted that Blank Rome advised J&J on certain issues that affected J&J affiliates:

> Pursuant to this Engagement Agreement, Blank Rome advised J&J on a variety of privacy matters, much of which was related to J&J affiliates. In particular, Jennifer Daniels, a partner at Blank Rome, provided affiliates with privacy-related services, including the preparation of policies and procedures, guidance documents, and training materials.[71]

The underlying action was a contract dispute between a J&J affiliate and a third party that Blank Rome also represented. However, Blank Rome did not advice the J&J affiliate and did not advise the third party when the parties entered into a contract.

The J&J affiliate was a wholly-owned subsidiary titled BabyCenter L.L.C. (BabyCenter). BabyCenter relied on J&J for a "variety of business services, including accounting, audit, cash management, employee benefits, finance, human resources, information technology, insurance, payroll, and travel services and systems."[72] BabyCenter also relied on J&J's legal department for either legal services or to provide outside counsel. Moreover, J&J exercised some degree of management control over BabyCenter.[73] What was not clear to the court, and was not clear from the opinion, was what degree of control J&J exercised and whether J&J's management control led to the underlying contract dispute.[74]

In 2006, BabyCenter entered into a five-year contract with GSI Commerce Solutions, Inc. (GSI). That contract provided that GSI would

---

68 *Id.*

69 *Id.*

70 *Id.* at 207.

71 *Id.*

72 *Id.*

73 *Id.* 207-08.

74 *Id.* at 208.

run the day-to-day operations of BabyCenter's online store. The contract also provided that in the event of a dispute the parties would first seek mediation then arbitration. In 2009, BabyCenter closed the online store and GSI claimed that BabyCenter wrongfully terminating the contract.[75] Blank Rome partners informed J&J of the dispute, but after mediation failed, BabyCenter informed Blank Rome that it would not proceed to arbitration as long as Blank Rome represented GSI.[76] Additionally, J&J informed Blank Rome that it opposed Blank Rome representing GSI.[77]

At trial, GSI attempted to compel arbitration, however, the court granted BabyCenter's motion to disqualify even though the court concluded that Blank Rome's separate representation of BabyCenter ended in 2006.[78] The district court analyzed the degree of control that J&J had over BabyCenter, and concluded that because of the operation control and because of BabyCenter's reliance on J&J's legal department, the two entities should be considered the same for disqualification purposes.[79] To add insult to injury, the district court also concluded that the initial agreement letter between J&J and Blank Rome did not give Blank Rome the authority to represent clients in actions against J&J affiliates.[80]

The Second Circuit began its analysis of whether a parent corporation and an affiliate should be considered the same for disqualification purposes by looking at comment 34 of ABA Model Rule 1.7.[81] The court also noted that two factors determine when a parent corporation and an affiliate should be considered as the same entity for disqualification: "(i) the degree of operational commonality between affiliated entities, and (ii) the extent to which one depends financially on the other."[82] As to operational commonality, courts had generally considered entities the same if the parent corporation and the affiliated entity shared technology systems, email systems, health plans, travel plans and computer net-

---

[75] *Id.*

[76] *Id.*

[77] *Id.*

[78] *Id.*

[79] *Id.* at 208-09.

[80] *Id.* at 209.

[81] *Id.* at 210.

[82] *Id.*

works.[83] For financial dependency, courts had found that parent corporations and affiliated entities should be the same entity when an adverse outcome would result in a substantial loss for the parent or when the affiliated entity is a wholly-owned subsidiary.

However, the Second Circuit disagreed with the conclusion that a wholly-owned subsidiary would automatically result in concluding that the parent and the subsidiary were the same entity.[84] The court supported this conclusion by citing an ABA Formal Ethics Opinion which stated that a parent corporation and a wholly-owned subsidiary should not be considered a single entity simply because the affiliated entity is wholly-owned by the parent.[85] Ultimately, the court concluded that because there was a substantial degree of "operational commonality" between J&J and BabyCenter, that the district court's decision to treat the entities as a single entity for disqualification purposes was justifiable.[86]

This conclusion is interesting because it illustrates how commonality exists between parent corporations and wholly-owned subsidiaries. J&J provided BabyCenter with accounting services, auditing services, cash management, employee benefits, finance, human resources, information technology, insurance, payroll and travel services and systems.[87] The two most important operational overlapping factors were the overlap between J&J's in-house legal department—which handled much of BabyCenter's legal affairs—and the fact that BabyCenter was a wholly-owned subsidiary that was subjected to some degree of managerial control.[88]

The facts in disqualification cases, like the cases addressed above, are interesting because these same facts would be relevant when determining whether a subsidiary was an alter ego of the parent corporation.[89] The next obvious question is whether a corporation would refrain from

---

[83] *Id.* at 210-11 (citing *Discotrade Ltd.*, 200 F.Supp.2d at 359; Eastman Kodak Co. v. Sony Corp., Nos. 04-CV-6095, 2004 WL 2984297, at *3-4 (W.D.N.Y. Dec. 27, 2004)).

[84] *Id.* at 211.

[85] *Id.* (citing American Bar Ass'n Comm. on Prof'l Ethics, Formal Opinion 95–390 at 1001:261–62).

[86] *Id.* at 211.

[87] *See id.*

[88] *See id.*

[89] *See, e.g.,* Phoenix Canada Oil Co. v. Texaco, Inc., 658 F. Supp. 1061, 1085 (D. Del. 1987), *aff'd*, 842 F.2d 1466 (3d Cir. 1988).

moving to disqualify opposing counsel because that motion may also open up the possibility for concluding that the subsidiary was the alter ego, or was merely the instrument of the parent corporation. However, none of the disqualification cases addressed above address the alter ego doctrine, suggesting that disqualification cases and alter ego cases are really focused on two different policy considerations, rather than just simply giving corporations protective benefits on both sides of the coin.

IV. Are These Policies Really at Odds?

Whether these two policies are odds is an interesting question because proponents against disqualification of counsel argue that corporations that do business with many affiliated entities must live with that decision and not benefit from an attorney's duty of loyalty.[90] Arguing that one policy is more important than the other assumes that the two policies cannot coexist. However, whether that assumption is true is not obvious from reviewing the cases analyzed in this chapter.

First, the duty of loyalty that lawyers owe clients stems is a policy consideration that aims at protecting the public and retaining public confidences in the legal profession.[91] Specifically, the duty of loyalty prevents a lawyer from using confidential information against a client in future adverse litigation.[92] This results in fostering more trust and confidence within the client-attorney relationship.[93] Without this duty, it is possible that a lawyer could learn something in confidence about their client, and then use that information against that client in future litigation if doing so was advantageous for the lawyer. This outcome would, theoretically, undermine public confidence in the legal system.[94]

On the other hand, limited liability structure and business associations are also deeply rooted legal traditions.[95] It is almost a common public understanding that parent corporations, in many situations, will not be liable for the acts of their subsidiary without demonstrating that

---

[90] Berman, ABA Annual Meeting, *supra* note 1.

[91] *See* FLAMM, LAWYER DISQUALIFICATION, *supra* note 5, at 247.

[92] *See id.*

[93] *Id.*

[94] *See id.*

[95] *See* 1 FLETCHER CYC. CORP., *supra* note 16, §§ 1-2.

the parent corporation dominated the subsidiary's actions.[96] However, the public policy at issue does not necessarily begin with keeping the parent corporation separate from a subsidiary.[97] The policy begins with keeping shareholders separate from the corporation.[98]

The idea is that corporations can take risks to grow the business without subjecting the shareholder to liability for the corporation's actions. Thus, if a party transacting with the corporation wanted to hold the shareholders liable for the corporations actions, that party would have to "pierce the corporate veil" to hold the shareholders liable.[99] Over time, corporations became shareholders in other corporations, and began wholly owning other corporations creating the parent-subsidiary relationship. Thus, if a party transacting with a subsidiary wants to hold the shareholders of the wholly-owned subsidiary responsible for the subsidiaries actions, then the party must, in some form, "pierce the corporate" veil to hold the shareholders liable.[100] Thus, as discussed above, a party would have to demonstrate through an "alter ego" or "instrumentality" test that the subsidiary was merely an instrument of the parent corporation, therefore it is really the parent corporation that is responsible for the resulting liabilities.[101]

If the issue is whether there are competing policy interests, then an answer requires placing the two interests against each other to see if the rules address the same policy concerns. If the two interests address the same policy concerns, then it is necessary to weigh the two interests against each other: either retain corporate liability structure and protect shareholders from being held personally liable for corporate wrongdoings, or allow corporations to disqualify counsel in circumstances where client confidences jeopardize the lawyer's duty of loyalty. The two policies clash when law firms represent parent corporations and then at some other point in time are retained to bring actions against the parent's

---

96 *See* United States Small Business Administration, "Corporations," https://www.sba.gov/starting-business/choose-your-business-structure/corporation (last visited April 26, 2017).

97 *See* 1 FLETCHER CYC. CORP., *supra* note 16, §§ 41-48.

98 *Id.*, § 25.

99 *Id.*, § 41.

100 *See id.*, §§ 41-48.

101 *See id.*

subsidiaries. Again, to illustrate the two policies again consider PepsiCo Inc. PepsiCo Inc. has 869 affiliated entities. PepsiCo is likely represented by a law firm, and by virtue of representing PepsiCo, that law firm may or may not represent any one of PepsiCo's affiliated entities, say, for example, Tropicana Inc. Specifically the clash is over whether PepsiCo should be allowed to disqualify its lawyers from representing some unrelated matter brought by its lawyers against Tropicana. Proponents arguing that no conflict of interest exists seemingly believe that it is simply unfair for PepsiCo to disqualify counsel when PepsiCo itself has declared that Tropicana is separate from PepsiCo regarding the entities duties and liabilities.

This raises the next question which is, what is unfair about a corporate client retaining its liability structure and receiving a duty of loyalty from its lawyers? It is important to remember that proponents that argue for a potential conflict of interest, argue that the conflict of interest is a fact sensitive inquiry with no presumption that a conflict of interest does, or does not, exist when a parent corporation moves to disqualify counsel. With that, what is unfair about corporations retaining their liability structure and receiving a duty of loyalty from their lawyers?

The answer is not obvious especially because none of the factors under the "alter ego" test or the "instrumentality" test address whether a centralized legal department is dispositive of a complete dominion of control.[102] Phrased alternatively, if a parent corporation held a centralized legal department for each of their affiliated entities, it is not clear whether that fact alone would demonstrate complete dominion over the affiliated entities. It is theoretically possible to conclude that a central legal department alone does not demonstrate complete dominion or control to discard the corporate structure because a central legal department would not manage the day-to-day activities over the subsidiary—which seems to be a very important factor in determining complete dominion.[103] Continuing with the PepsiCo example, if PepsiCo had a central legal department that provided legal counsel to all of PepsiCo's 869 affiliated entities, including Tropicana, a court would likely find that fact as evidence of PepsiCo's control over the affiliated entities. But what if a court also found

---

[102] *See id.; see also* Phoenix Canada Oil Co. v. Texaco, Inc., 658 F. Supp. 1061, 1085 (D. Del. 1987), *aff'd*, 842 F.2d 1466 (3d Cir. 1988).

[103] *See Phoenix Canada Oil Co.*, 658 F. Supp. at 1085.

that Tropicana was in charge of its own day-to-day operations such as hiring and firing employees, managing schedules, keeping their own books and paying their own taxes? These factors would likely point towards concluding that the degree of PepsiCo's control over Tropicana not total and complete, therefore a court would likely not discard the corporate structure.

On the other hand, if a law firm representing a parent corporation had information about an affiliated entity by virtue of representing the parent corporation, then it is possible that the law firm could use that information in adverse litigation against the affiliated entity if it was advantageous for the law firm to do so—and this is exactly what conflict of interest rules aim to protect against.[104] To use the PepsiCo example again, it may be advantageous for a law firm representing PepsiCo to use information about PepsiCo's business if the law firm was asked to bring a suit against Tropicana. Thus, to the extent that the two policy issues cannot coexist, is it more important to protect PepsiCo's confidential information from being used against Tropicana in a lawsuit, or is it more important to discard the corporate structure and always declare that Tropicana and PepsiCo are the same entity?

V. Conclusion

Retaining corporate liability structure to protect shareholders from being held personally liable does not obviously address the same public policy concerns that lawyer ethical duties protect against. Specifically, whether a parent corporation is liable for the wrongdoings of its affiliated entity is an entirely different question than whether a parent corporation can disqualify their lawyer for breaching the duty of loyalty that the lawyer owed the corporation. With no clear answer, it seems that always finding no conflict of interest could theoretically allow lawyers to violate their duty of loyalty to the parent corporation if it were in the lawyer's interest to do so. For that reason, it seems that attorneys potentially violating their duty of loyalty to their clients is a greater public risk than allowing parent corporations, as shareholders, to retain separateness from any of their affiliated entities.

---

104 *See* FLAMM, LAWYER DISQUALIFICATION, *supra* note 5, at 247.

This conclusion agrees with a formal ethics opinion issued by the ABA in 1995, "in which a divided ethics committee concluded that representation of one company in a corporate family does not necessarily disqualify the firm from representing a client in an unrelated matter against the parent, subsidiary, or affiliate of the first company."[105] The question that this chapter addresses is not exactly easy to imagine conceptually as illustrated by the divided ethics committee opinion from over twenty years ago. Moreover, the modern reality is corporations continue to grow and become more complex. For that reason alone, it would be impractical and unwise to conclude that representing a parent corporation with hundreds of affiliated entities creates a conflict of interest when the representing attorney brings an action against one of the affiliated entities without determining whether an actual conflict exists.

---

[105] Berman, ABA Annual Meeting, *supra* note 1 (citing ABA Formal Ethics Opinion 95-390).

2

Prosecutorial Misconduct and Wrongful Convictions: A Plague Upon Our Criminal Justice System?

Jessica Dennis

I. Introduction

In 1985, John Thompson was prosecuted by Orleans Parish in New Orleans, Louisiana for murder and attempted robbery.[1] During the course of this investigation and trial a blood analysis was done.[2] However, this evidence was not disclosed to Thompson's attorney and instead was suppressed all through trial.[3] This led to his conviction for both crimes.[4] After eighteen years in prison, fourteen of which was spent on death row, this analysis was uncovered.[5] Thompson's blood type did not match the blood from the analysis and his death sentence was eventually overturned.[6]

In March 2006, a woman accused three lacrosse players from Duke of kidnapping and raping her.[7] This story of kidnap and rape turned out to be completely fabricated, either a hoax or a false allegation that was based on a delusion.[8] The prosecutor in that case was aware that the "victim" was lying.[9] A year later, in April 2007, the Attorney General of North Carolina dropped all of the charges.[10] Two months later, in June 2007, the

---

[1] Connick v. Thompson, 563 U.S. 51, ___, 131 S. Ct. 1350, 1356 (2011).

[2] *Id.*

[3] *Id.*

[4] *Id.*

[5] *Id.*

[6] *Id.*

[7] Robert P. Mosteller, *The Duke Lacrosse Case, Innocence, and False Identifications: A Fundamental Failure to "Do Justice,"* 76 FORDHAM L. REV. 1337, 1338 (2007).

[8] *Id.*

[9] *Id.*

[10] *Id.* at 1337.

original prosecutor on the case was disbarred for not only withholding exculpatory evidence, but for partaking in prejudicial pretrial publicity.[11]

Mark Collin Sodersten was convicted in California of the special circumstance murder of Julie Watson.[12] Sodersten was sentenced to life in prison without the possibility for parole.[13] Twelve years after Sodersten's conviction, during a habeas corpus proceeding, it was uncovered that prosecuting and law enforcement authorities were aware of or actually possessed recorded statements from the two key trial witnesses at the time of trial.[14] The recordings contained inconsistent statements in addition to an admission of lying and the coercive interrogation of one witness.[15] The defense never knew of these recordings as they were not ever disclosed to the defense.[16] Sodersten ended up serving twenty-two years and died in prison six months prior to his conviction being reversed.[17]

In 1986 Michael Morton's wife, Christine, was beaten to death in their home in Texas.[18] The jury convicted Morton of Christine's murder.[19] The prosecutor in the case failed to turn over exculpatory evidence and Morton was later exonerated by DNA evidence.[20]

All of the cases mentioned above have one similarity: individuals were treated unfairly in the criminal justice system due to the misconduct of the prosecutorial team. While prosecutorial misconduct is not happening in every single case it does exist. The very existence of this type of behavior goes against the ideal of justice and fairness in our criminal justice system that the Supreme Court has held so dear. The American criminal justice system displays its worst qualities when any individual

---

[11] *Id.*

[12] *In re* Sodersten, 146 Cal. App. 4th 1163, 1169 (2007).

[13] *Id.*

[14] *Id.*

[15] *Id.*

[16] *Id.*

[17] *Id.* at 1218-19.

[18] Morton v. Texas, 761 S.W.2d 876, 876 (Tex. Ct. App. 1988); *see also Ex parte* Morton, No. AP-76663, 2011 WL 4827841, at *1 (Tex. Crim. App. Oct. 12, 2011) (per curiam).

[19] *Morton*, 761 S.W.2d at 876.

[20] *Id.*

who stands accused of a crime is treated unfairly.[21] However, the American criminal justice system has also shown some of its best qualities when both sides adhere to the rules and create a fair and balanced trial.[22]

Unfortunately, the criminal justice system often falls short of its best for a number of reasons. In this chapter, I will look at the relationship of ethical violations and wrongful convictions. In Part II of this chapter, I will identify the contributing factors to wrongful convictions. In Part III, I will identify the types of ethical violations, specifically prosecutorial misconduct, that occur most often in our criminal justice system. In Part IV, I will look at the intersection of those ethical violations and wrongful convictions as a whole.

II. The Ethical Duty of a Prosecutor

The rule that specifically addresses and governs the special responsibilities of a prosecuting attorney is Model Rule 3.8.[23] These special responsibilities of a prosecuting attorney include making "timely disclosure to the defense of all evidence or information known to the prosecutor that tends to negate the guilt of the accused or mitigates the offense"—in other words, *Brady* violations.[24] Further, the rule states that if a prosecuting attorney finds new, credible, and material evidence that creates a reasonable likelihood that a convicted defendant did not commit the offense, the prosecutor must disclose that evidence to an appropriate authority and the defendant.[25]

The comments that accompany the rule mention the predominant principles that govern prosecutorial ethics.[26] Comment one describes the role of the prosecuting attorney as that of "a minister of justice and not simply that of an advocate," including "specific obligations to see that the

---

[21] Brady v. Maryland, 373 U.S. 83, 87 (1963) ("Society wins not only when the guilty are convicted but when criminal trials are fair. . . .").

[22] *Id.*

[23] AMERICAN BAR ASS'N, MODEL RULES OF PROF'L CONDUCT r. 3.8 (2003). The states have implemented this requirement in their own codes of conduct based on the ABA's model rule.

[24] *Id.*, r. 3.8(d); *see Brady*, 373 U.S. 83 (1963).

[25] AMERICAN BAR ASS'N, MODEL RULES OF PROF'L CONDUCT r. 3.8(g) (2003).

[26] AMERICAN BAR ASS'N, MODEL RULES OF PROF'L CONDUCT r. 3.8 cmt. 1 (2003).

defendant is accorded procedural justice and that guilt is decided upon the basis of sufficient evidence."[27] The ABA has a similar standard in its Criminal Justice Standards on the Prosecutorial Function.[28] The standard famously provides that the "duty of a prosecutor is to seek justice, not merely to convict."[29] The National District Attorneys Association has published its own Prosecution Standards.[30] This standard cautions prosecuting attorneys to always be "vigilant when the accused may be innocent."[31]

Unfortunately, this rule does not directly address many of the issues that will be discussed in this chapter. However, several of the rules that are directed at all attorneys are applicable to the solicitation and presentation of jailhouse informants and dishonest experts,[32] both topics that will be covered. But, very few of these rules provide bright line rules to prosecuting attorneys about the specific obligations that they have concerning these type of highly suspect witnesses.[33] For example, Rule 8.4 states that it is professional misconduct for an attorney to engage in conduct involving dishonesty, fraud, deceit, or misrepresentation.[34] It is also professional misconduct for an attorney to "engage in conduct that is prejudicial to the administration of justice."[35] However, the comments to this rule provide no clue of its potential reach in the context of prosecutorial obligations that concern the engagement of witnesses who may be lying.[36] It is unlikely that the rule will provide additional constraints to the prevailing directives that already prohibit attorneys from knowingly

---

[27] *Id.*

[28] STANDARDS FOR CRIMINAL JUSTICE: PROSECUTION FUNCTION AND DEFENSE FUNCTION STANDARD 3-1.2(c) (3d ed. 1993).

[29] *Id.*

[30] NATIONAL PROSECUTION STANDARD (Nat'l Dist. Atty's Ass'n, 2d ed. 1991).

[31] *Id.* § 68.4.

[32] Myrna S. Raeder, *See No Evil: Wrongful Convictions and the Prosecutorial Ethics of Offering Testimony by Jailhouse Informants and Dishonest Experts*, 76 FORDHAM L. REV. 1413, 1429 (2007).

[33] *Id.*

[34] AMERICAN BAR ASS'N, MODEL RULE OF PROF'L CONDUCT r. 8.4(c) (2003).

[35] *Id.,* r. 8.4(d).

[36] Raeder, *supra* note 32.

"making a false statement of fact or law to a tribunal" or "offering evidence that the lawyer knows to be false."[37]

An attorney is also not able to "falsify evidence, counsel or assist a witness to testify falsely, or offer an inducement to a witness that is prohibited by law."[38] However, none of the rules or standards that are provided to prosecuting attorneys directly speak to many of the issues that face prosecutors during their everyday practice. This leaves a huge gap allowing prosecutors complete discretion in an area that should arguably be closely supervised.

III. Leading Causes of Wrongful Convictions

The institutional and societal view that prosecutors have the primary goal to gain convictions has persisted in the minds of citizens despite the evidence that wrongful convictions have been occurring at an alarming rate and with disturbing regularity in the United States.[39] This accepted idea that the American prosecutor is and should be principally concerned with acquiring and maintaining convictions not only causes the innocent to be convicted, but also makes it nearly impossible for an individual who has been wrongfully convicted to gain their freedom (an already over-whelming and discouraging undertaking in perfect circumstances).[40] Once an individual has been convicted it becomes progressively harder for the legitimacy of that result to be critically examined.[41] Appellate courts are extremely limited in the issues that they may address in an appeal and

---

37 AMERICAN BAR ASS'N, MODEL RULES OF PROF'L CONDUCT r. 3.3(a)(1), (3) (2003).

38 *Id.,* r. 3.4(b).

39 Daniel S. Medwed, *The Prosecutor as Minister of Justice: Preaching to the Unconverted from the Post-Conviction Pulpit,* 84 WASH. L. REV. 35, 36 (2009) [hereinafter Medwed, *Minister of Justice*]; *see also* Matt Ferner, *A Record Number of People Were Exonerated in 2015 for Crimes They Didn't Commit,* WASHINGTON POST (February 3, 2016, 12:02 A.M.), http://www.huffingtonpost.com/entry/exonerations-2015_us_56ac0374e4b00b033aaf3da9; Samuel R. Gross, *The Staggering Number of Wrongful Convictions in America,* WASHINGTON POST (July 24, 2015), https://www.washingtonpost.com/opinions/the-cost-of-convicting-the-innocent/2015/07/24/260fc3a2-1aae-11e5-93b7-5eddc056ad8a_story.html?utm_term=.e4149bb67eb3

40 Medwed, *Minister of Justice, supra* note 39.

41 *Id.*

generally restrict themselves to only those issues and topics that were presented to the judge at trial.[42]

As a result, the daunting task of evaluating claims of actual innocence typically falls into the realm of the collateral post-conviction process (e.g., writs of habeas corpus, corum nobis, or statutory analogues).[43] States have been infamously skeptical and suspicious of post-conviction innocence claims that are based on newly discovered evidence.[44] This distrust and disfavor is made apparent through the post-conviction procedures.[45] These procedures include rigorous statutes of limitations, arduous burdens of proof, and deferential standards of appellate review.[46]

Since 1989 there have been 2,020[47] exonerations in the United States.[48] That averages out to roughly seventy-one people per year: 2,020 individuals who have been determined to be innocent of the crimes that they were charged with and convicted of; 2,020 individuals who have spent part of their lives, precious time they could have spent with loved

---

[42] *See, e.g.*, URSULA BENTELE & EVE CARY, APPELLATE ADVOCACY: PRINCIPLES AND PRACTICE 77 (4th ed. 2004) ("At all levels of appellate review, it is a fundamental rule that the appellate court is bound strictly by the record of the evidence adduced in the trial court. . . . The next most important limitation on an appellate court's scope of review is the general rule that any legal issue raised on appeal must have been 'preserved.' That is, the issue must first have been presented to the trial court.").

[43] *See generally* Daniel S. Medwed, *California Dreaming? The Golden State's Restless Approach to Newly Discovered Evidence of Innocence*, 40 U.C. DAVIS L. REV. 1437 (2007) [hereinafter Medwed, *California Dreaming*] (discussing California's approach to post-conviction innocence claims based on newly discovered non-DNA evidence); *see also* Daniel S. Medwed, *Introduction to Beyond Biology: Wrongful Convictions in the Post-DNA World*, 2008 UTAH L. REV. 1 (2008) (introducing a symposium on wrongful convictions unrelated to DNA evidence); Daniel S. Medwed, *Up the River Without a Procedure: Innocent Prisoners and Newly Discovered Non-DNA Evidence in State Courts,* 47 ARIZ. L. REV. 655 (2005) [hereinafter Medwed, *Up the River*] (analyzing state approaches to newly discovered non-DNA evidence claims); Kathy Swedlow, *Don't Believe Everything You Read: A Review of Modern "Post-Conviction" DNA Testing Statutes*, 38 CAL. W. L. REV. 355, 382-84 (2002) (critiquing state post-conviction statutes governing DNA testing).

[44] *See, e.g.*, People v. Sutton, 73 Cal. 243, 248 (1887) (suggesting that claims of newly discovered evidence should be "regarded with distrust and disfavor").

[45] Medwed, *Up the River, supra* note 43 (describing the procedures through which post-conviction claims of innocence are typically litigated in state courts).

[46] *Id.*

[47] This number of exonerations is accurate as of April 27, 2017.

[48] The National Registry of Exonerations, https://www.law.umich.edu/special/ exoneration/Pages/browse.aspx?View={b8342ae7-6520-4a32-8a06-4b326208baf8} &SortField=Exonerated&SortDir=Desc&FilterClear=1 [hereinafter National Registry].

ones, locked up behind bars for a crime that they did not commit. If this number does not startle you, perhaps consider the fact that 1,033 of those convictions were due to "official misconduct."[49] While there are many different factors (all of which often times overlap in any given case) that contribute to wrongful convictions, which I will discuss below, "official misconduct" is arguably the scariest factor. If one cannot even trust those whose duty it is to honor the letter and spirit of the law, then whom can one trust?

A. Perjury or False Accusation

According to The National Registry of Exonerations, perjury or false accusation is one of the contributing factors to wrongful convictions.[50] Perjury or false accusations occur when an individual has been falsely accused of committing a crime for which the individual was later exonerated.[51] This perjury or false accusation can occur either in sworn testimony or otherwise, for example, talking to law enforcement.[52] This contributing factor accounts for 1,139 of the total 2,020 wrongful convictions since 1989.[53]

B. False or Misleading Forensic Evidence

The next contributing factor that is listed is false or misleading forensic evidence.[54] This occurs when a conviction is based, at least in part, on forensic evidence that was (1) caused by errors in testing, (2) based on unreliable or unproven methods, (3) expressed with exaggerated and misleading confidences, or (4) fraudulent.[55] This contributing factor accounts for 480 of the 2,020 wrongful convictions since 1989.[56]

---

49 *Id.*

50 *Id.*

51 The National Registry of Exonerations, Glossary, https://www.law.umich.edu/special/exoneration/Pages/glossary.aspx [hereinafter Glossary].

52 *Id.*

53 National Registry, *supra* note 48.

54 *Id.*

55 Glossary, *supra* note 51.

56 National Registry, *supra* note 48.

C. Official Misconduct

Another contributing factor is official misconduct.[57] Official Misconduct is classified as the police, prosecutors, or other government official significantly abusing their authority or the judicial process in a manner that contributed to the conviction of the individual.[58] As mentioned above, this contributing factor makes up 1,033 of the total 2,020 cases of wrongful convictions since 1989.[59] While this is not the highest factor, it is very nearly the most common factor and could easily take the lead. This factor is definitely one of the most alarming in my opinion. This factor encompasses many of the ethical violations that prosecutors face (discussed in Part III of this chapter). This factor encompasses misconduct from the very people who have sworn to not only obey, but uphold the law in every aspect, something that seems to pose some difficulty according to the statistics.

D. Inadequate Legal Defense

The next contributing factor is inadequate legal defense.[60] This occurs when a defense attorney provided obviously and grossly inadequate representation to an individual.[61] This contributing factor makes up 476 of the total 2,020 cases of wrongful convictions since 1989.[62] It is likely that this contributing factor encompasses many of the post-conviction relief actions, such as ineffective assistance of counsel.

---

57 *Id.*

58 Glossary, *supra* note 51; *see also* JIM DWYER, PETER NEUFELD & BARRY SCHECK, ACTUAL INNOCENCE: FIVE DAYS TO EXECUTION AND OTHER DISPATCHES FROM THE WRONGLY CONVICTED, app. 2 (2000) (analyzing DNA exonerations in the U.S. by state, factors leading to wrongful convictions, examples of mistaken identity, prosecutorial and police misconduct, incarceration, and race of both victim and defendant).

59 National Registry, *supra* note 48; *see also* DWYER, NEUFELD & SCHECK, *supra* note 58.

60 *Id.*

61 Glossary, *supra* note 51.

62 National Registry, *supra* note 48.

E. Mistaken Witness Identification

The next contributing factor is mistaken witness identification.[63] This occurs when at least one of the witnesses from the trial mistakenly identified the individual as a person that the witness saw committing the crime in question.[64] This contributing factor makes up 597 of the total 2,020 cases of wrongful convictions since 1989.[65] While it is unlikely that these mistaken identifications are done out of malice or with the direct intention of placing an innocent person behind bars, it is still a sad fact that it does happen and has contributed to innocent individuals being convicted.

F. False Confession

The next contributing factor is false confessions.[66] An individual falsely confesses when (1) he or she made a false statement to authorities which was treated as a confession, (2) the authorities claimed that the individual made such statements but the individual denies it, or (3) the individual made a statement that was not an admission of guilt, but was misinterpreted as such by authorities.[67] This contributing factor makes up 244 of the total 2,020 cases of wrongful conviction since 1989.[68] This type of contributing factor could be coerced out of an individual or the statement could be used out of context to illicit a certain result during a trial. However, it does not appear that this is a common occurrence, or it is well hidden if it is.

---

[63] *Id.*

[64] Glossary, *supra* note 51.

[65] National Registry, *supra* note 48; *see also* Daniel Medwed, *Anatomy of a Wrongful Conviction: Theoretical Implications and Practical Solutions*, 51 VILL. L.REV. 337, 358 (2006) ("Virtually all of the pertinent studies since 1932 have pinpointed eyewitness misidentification as the single most pervasive factor in the conviction of the innocent.").

[66] *Id.*

[67] Glossary, *supra* note 51.

[68] National Registry, *supra* note 48.

G. Jailhouse Informant

Although The National Registry of Exonerations does not list the jailhouse informant as a contributing factor, it is listed in the glossary.[69] A jailhouse informant is an individual, a witness in the trial, who was incarcerated with the individual defendant.[70] This informant testifies or reports that the defendant confessed the crime to him or her.[71] The Registry does not list this as an individual contributing factor and as a result there is no specific data about how this plays a role in the cases of wrongful convictions. It could be that the Registry encompasses the use of jailhouse informants in another category, such as official misconduct. However, I will discuss below how jailhouse informants can be used by the prosecution to illicit certain results and the possible ethical violations with the use of such witnesses. Further, I will discuss why jailhouse informants are not a reliable source of information.

IV. Common Ethical Violations among Prosecutors

In the American criminal justice system there is institutional and societal acceptance of the view that the primary goal of a prosecuting attorney is "to convict."[72] This publicly accepted idea that the American prosecutor is and should be principally concerned with acquiring and maintaining convictions—contrary to the actual ethical duty to seek justice—not only causes the innocent to be convicted, but also makes it nearly impossible for an individual who has been wrongfully convicted to

---

[69] Glossary, *supra* note 51.

[70] *Id.*

[71] *Id.*; *see also* George C. Thomas, III, *When Lawyers Fail Innocent Defendants: Exorcising the Ghosts That Haunt the Criminal Justice Systems*, 2008 UTAH L.REV. 25, 29 (2008) (discussing the percentage of exonerations that lying informants contributed to); DWYER, NEUFELD & SCHECK, *supra* note 59; JIM DWYER, PETER NEUFELD & BARRY SCHECK, ACTUAL INNOCENCE: WHEN JUSTICE GOES WRONG AND HOW TO MAKE IT RIGHT 361 (2001) (noting that, out of the first 74 DNA exonerations, 19% of the convictions involved "informants/snitches"). *See generally* Northwestern Univ. Sch. of Law Ctr. on Wrongful Convictions, "The Snitch System: How Snitch Testimony Sent Randy Steidle and Other Innocent American to Death Row" (2004), http://www .law.northwestern.edu/wrongfulconvictions/documents/SnitchSystemBooklet.pdf [hereinafter "Snitch System"].

[72] Medwed, *Minister of Justice*, *supra* note 39.

gain their freedom (an already overwhelming and discouraging undertaking in perfect circumstances).[73]

A. *Brady Violations*

> "There is an epidemic of *Brady* violations abroad in the land.
> Only judges can put a stop to it."[74]

Over fifty years ago the United States Supreme Court decided a landmark case, *Brady v. Maryland*,[75] launching the modern rule of prosecutorial disclosure requirements that are designed to uphold the due process guarantees of the Fourteenth Amendment.[76] The Forty-second Congress introduced a statute designed to target misconduct by government officials.[77] This statute provides a remedy for individual rights and protections that are secured by the Fourteenth Amendment.[78] This statutory protection combined with the Court's decision in *Brady*[79] highlighted the common goal of both the judiciary and the legislature: fairness for individuals accused by the authorities who have the power to ensure it.[80]

In *Brady*,[81] the Supreme Court spelled out the role that the prosecutor plays in promoting the constitutional due process rights of an accused individual. In this case, the accused individual discovered that the prosecutor had failed to disclose the confession of an accomplice to the

---

[73] *Id.*

[74] United States v. Olsen, 737 F.3d 625, 626 (9th Cir. 2013) (Kozinski, C.J., dissenting from denial of rehearing en banc).

[75] Brady v. Maryland, 373 U.S. 83 (1963).

[76] U.S. Const. Amend. XIV, § 1; *see Brady*, 373 U.S. at 87 ("The suppression by the prosecution of evidence favorable to an accused upon request violates due process where the evidence is material either to guilt or to punishment, irrespective of the good faith or bad faith of the prosecution.").

[77] *See* 42 U.S.C. § 1983 (2006); *see generally* Melissa Lawson Romero, Comment, *Connick v. Thompson: Forsaking Constitutional Due Process for Fear of Flooding Litigation and Loss of Municipal Autonomy*, 89 DENV. U.L. REV. 771, 771 (2012).

[78] *Id.*

[79] 373 U.S. 83 (1963).

[80] Romero, Comment, *supra* note 77.

[81] 373 U.S. 83 (1963).

homicide after he had admitted that he had participated in the murder himself.[82] The Court determined that this act of suppressing the evidence violated the constitutional due process rights of the accused individual.[83] The Court then announced the current rule, a much needed reform, of discovery and mandatory disclosures.[84] "[T]he suppression by the prosecution of evidence favorable to an accused upon request violates due process where the evidence is material to guilt or punishment, irrespective of the good faith or bad faith of the prosecution."[85] This new rule emphasized the judiciary's commitment to justice and fair play in the criminal justice system.

Since the landmark decision in 1963, the Brady rule has undergone substantial judicial facelifts.[86] Some of the most noteworthy of the revisions include the elimination of the need for an accused individual to specifically request Brady evidence,[87] the requirement of disclosure in cases of both exculpatory and impeachment evidence,[88] and the amplification of the importance of not distinguishing between the good and bad faith of the prosecutor.[89] However, one of the most obvious modifications to the Brady rule has to do with the judiciary's retrospective interpretation of the concept of "materiality."[90] A piece of evidence is only considered material when there is a reasonable probability that had the evidence been disclosed to the defense, the result of the proceeding would have

---

[82] *Id.* at 84.

[83] *Id.* at 86-87.

[84] *Id.*

[85] *Id.* at 87.

[86] Romero, *supra* note 77, at 775.

[87] *See* Bennet L. Gershman, *Reflections on Brady v. Maryland*, 47 S. Tex. L. Rev. 685, 704-06 (2006) (referencing and discussing the holding in *United States v. Bagley*, 473 U.S. 667 (1985)).

[88] *See id.* at 702.

[89] *See, e.g.*, United States v. Agurs, 427 U.S. 97, 110 n.17 (1979).

[90] *See, e.g.*, United States v. Oxman, 740 F.2d 1298, 1310 (3d Cir. 1984) (noting the "tendency to adopt a retrospective view of materiality"); United States v. Coppa, 267 F.3d 132, 140 (2d Cir. 2001) ("the scope of the defendant's constitutional right . . . is ultimately defined retrospectively, by reference to the likely effect that the suppression of particular evidence had on the outcome of the trial"); Gershman, *supra* note 87, at 689.

been different.[91] This evaluation of materiality has afforded prosecutors with a wide discretion in their determination of what constitutes Brady evidence and then often results in the inconsistent application of the rule.[92] Not only can it be difficult for a prosecutor to know what should be disclosed under Brady, but it can be extremely difficult for a defense attorney to request such evidence, as by its very nature the defense has no idea what this evidence could be.

B. Use of Jailhouse Informants

> "The most dangerous informer of all is the jailhouse snitch
> who claims another prisoner has confessed to him."[93]

Jailhouse informants have been identified as a leading cause of wrongful convictions for quite some time.[94] When a claim is brought in regards to prosecutions and convictions involving jailhouse informants the accused individual generally will allege a number of complaints. These complaints generally include that the prosecutor knowingly introduced perjured or false testimony,[95] the prosecutor did not correct false testimony,[96] or that the prosecutor failed to disclose exculpatory Brady material.[97]

---

91 United States v. Bagley, 473 U.S. 667, 678 (1985); *see also* Kyles v. Whitley, 514 U.S. 419, 434 (1995) (refining the *Bagley* standard holding that a showing of materiality depends on "whether in its absence [the defendant] received a fair trial, understood as the trial resulting in a verdict worthy of confidence").

92 *See, e.g., Thompson*, 553 F.3d at 853 (5th Cir. 2008) (noting "the difficulty in interpreting *Brady*" and the common understanding that *Brady* is a "'gray' area, subject to interpretation"), *rev'd*, 563 U.S. 51, 131 S. Ct. 1350 (2011); *see also Thompson*, 563 U.S. at ___, 131 S. Ct. at 1365 (acknowledging that "*Brady* has gray areas and some *Brady* decisions are difficult").

93 Stephen S. Trott, *Words of Warning for Prosecutors Using Criminals as Witnesses*, 47 HASTINGS L.J. 1381, 1394 (1996).

94 *See, e.g.,* DWYER, NEUFELD & SCHECK, *supra* note 71. *See generally* "Snitch System," *supra* note 71.

95 *See, e.g.,* Mooney v. Holohan, 294 U.S. 103, 110 (1935).

96 *See, e.g.,* Napue v. Illinois, 360 U.S. 264, 265 (1959).

97 *Brady*, 373 U.S. at 87 (holding "that the suppression of evidence by the prosecution favorable to an accused upon request violates due process where the evidence is material either to guilt or to punishment, irrespective of the good or bad faith of the prosecution").

Because of the very nature of our adversarial system and the fact that prosecutors generally offer leniency in exchange for testimony from individuals with knowledge of the crime, even if they were involved themselves, there has been a trend of the use of jailhouse informants. Often times because the individual is aware that their credibility is very low they will go so far as to bring others into their plans and fabricate corroborations for their false testimony.[98] Jailhouse informants arguably pose the greatest threat to the veracity of the American criminal justice system.[99] During the course of an investigation into the causes of wrongful convictions a Canadian commission stated that "jailhouse informants comprise the most deceitful and deceptive group of witnesses known to frequent the courts. . . . They are smooth and convincing liars."[100]

Jailhouse informers generally have no insider knowledge of the crime.[101] Therefore, the only the only basis for the jailhouse informers to receive any better treatment or their freedom is through alleged confessions that were made to them by the accused.[102] The nation, while watching an interview of Leslie Vernon White on 60 minutes, was shocked to learn how easy it is to fabricate a confession without ever having any contact with the accused individual.[103] White admitted to committing perjury multiple times during her time as a jailhouse informant.[104] According to White, the "snitch" system had spawn slogans, such as "don't go to the pen, send a friend" and "if you can't do the time, just drop a dime."[105] The amount of access that inmates and/or their friends have to the internet, media, and cell phones has amplified the

---

[98] Northern Mariana Islands v. Bowie, 243 F.3d 1109, 1124 (9th Cir. 2001).

[99] Raeder, *supra* note 32, at 1419.

[100] Manitoba Justice, "The Inquiry Regarding Thomas Sophonow: Jailhouse Informants, Their Unreliablity and the Importance of Complete Crown Disclosure Pertaining to Them" (2001), https://digitalcollection.gov.mb.ca/awweb/pdfopener ?smd=1&did=12713&md=1

[101] Raeder, *supra* note 32, at 1419.

[102] *Id.*

[103] "Snitch System," *supra* note 71, at 2; *see also* Raeder, *supra* note 32, at 1419 (further discussing the "snitch system" and the effect and involvement of jailhouse informants).

[104] *Id.*

[105] *Id.*

ability of those inmates to obtain the type of information that sounds like it would be insider knowledge.[106]

The leniency provided to jailhouse informants is so great, providing the jailhouse informants with a high incentive to lie with the possibility of minimal consequences.[107] Thus, prosecutorial reliance upon this type of witness provides an ethical challenge for the prosecutor.[108] The trustworthiness and honesty of jailhouse informants is inherently suspect, unless there is a recording of the conversation and the confession is actually captured on tape.[109] Jailhouse informants do not only come forward when a prosecuting attorney asks them to come forward.[110] Jailhouse informants are willing to pawn their claims that an accused individual confessed to them by their cellmates, someone sitting next to them on the bus to court, or high-profile individuals who passed by them in the yard or cafeteria.[111] It seems that beyond the benefits that a jailhouse informant receives for their testimony, there is also a sense of thrill or entertainment for the jailhouse informant, otherwise why volunteer such information and go to such lengths to fabricate such elaborate confessions?

Prosecutors are in the unique position that allows them to know the prior history of the jailhouse informant.[112] Prosecutors are also privy to the benefits that a jailhouse informant is receiving or that have been offered.[113] They can also test the veracity of the jailhouse informant's

---

[106] Raeder, *supra* note 32, at 1419.

[107] *Id.*; *see also* Thomas, *supra* note 71, at 29-30 (discussing how little the Supreme Court has done to ensure that jailhouse informants are telling the truth and the potential for innocent people to be convicted when prosecutors are willing to offer extremely generous deals while ignoring the possibility that the informant is lying).

[108] Raeder, *supra* note 32, at 1419.

[109] *Id.* at 1419-20; *see also* Steve Mills & Ken Armstrong, *The Failure of the Death Penalty in Illinois: The Inside Informant*, CHI. TRIB., Nov. 16, 1999, at 1 (noting that a jailhouse informant taped defendant for six hours with a recorder supplied by the Federal Bureau of Investigations and, in spite of the absence of an alleged confession from the recordings due to claimed malfunctions, the prosecution offered the testimony on the theory that the informant knew private details of the crime, although a different prosecutor called the jailhouse informant a pathological liar).

[110] Raeder, *supra* note 32, at 1420.

[111] *Id.*

[112] *Id.* at 1437.

[113] *Id.*

claims as well as take steps to corroborate the testimony.[114] However, it seems that often times these measures are not taken and jailhouse informants are used when their testimony is not exactly truthful, leading to an increase in innocent individuals being accused, convicted, and incarcerated based upon this seemingly damning testimony.

C. Use of Unreliable Expert Testimony

Similar to jailhouse informants, dishonest expert witnesses have been identified as a substantial cause of wrongful convictions.[115] Prosecutors should be wary of the testimony from questionable experts.[116] Testimony from questionable experts carry a high likelihood that they are false.[117] Although it could be easy to confuse incompetent experts with dishonest experts, they are very different. Dishonest experts include the prosecuting attorney "shopping" around for an expert that agrees with their desired conclusion, experts who describe problematic techniques using statistical comparison that are not based in fact, experts who conclude something that none of their colleagues can duplicate, and experts who simply lie about their qualifications or their findings.[118]

When a prosecuting attorney goes "expert shopping" in order to find an expert with a favorable conclusion which cannot be duplicated, the prosecution should then be put on notice that the testimony of the expert is potentially falsified.[119] There is also a danger with using testimony from an expert who presents statistics that are not based on reliable tech-

---

114 *Id.* For example, prosecutors routinely use polygraphs for investigative purposes, although the evidence is not typically admissible at trial. In this regard, a finding that the jailhouse informant is lying should disqualify him because the risk he is actually lying is so great. In contrast, a finding of truthfulness should not automatically qualify the jailhouse informant in light of other factors, such as a previous perjury conviction or lack of strong corroboration.

115 *See, e.g.,* DWYER, NEUFELD & SCHECK, *supra* note 71, at 361 (noting that, out of the first 74 DNA exonerations, 34% involved defective or fraudulent science).

116 Raeder, *supra* note 32, at 1415.

117 *Id.*

118 *Id.; see, e.g.,* Bennett L. Gershman, *Misuse of Scientific Evidence by Prosecutors,* 28 OKLA. CITY U.L.REV. 17, 32 (2003) (discussing fabricated statistics concerning a hair analysis and concluding that the results were so far-fetched that they suggest the prosecution made a conscious effort to obtain a conviction based on manufactured testimony with the expert's assistance).

119 Raeder, *supra* note 32, at 1420.

niques.[120] These experts are often referred to as being "prosecution friendly," arguably capturing the bias and coloring the expert's evaluation of the evidence.[121]

V. The Intersection of Prosecutorial Misconduct and Wrongful Convictions

As I have mentioned in Part II, there are very few rules governing the specific behavior of prosecuting attorneys. It appears that there is a lot of discretion on the part of prosecuting attorneys when it comes to what evidence to put forward or provide to the other side, which witnesses to use, and what experts to put on the stand. However, this complete control and discretion over cases does not come for free.

The number of wrongful convictions in the United States is startling. As noted above, since 1989 there have been 2,020.[122] While it is nearly impossible for us to ever know the true number of all wrongful convictions in our nation, approximately 1.4 percent of convicted individuals that are sentenced to death in the United States are later shown to be innocent.[123] That means every one in twenty-five capital convictions is incorrect and sends an innocent person to jail, or worse.[124] It is very difficult to know the exact number of wrongful convictions in lesser offenses, however, those who are convicted of capital crimes are better documented, providing us with this base number of wrongful convictions.[125] While it would be impractical, improper, and just incorrect to say that every single one of these cases of wrongful convictions is due to some misconduct on the part of the prosecuting attorney, it is not unreasonable to think that the alarmingly high rate of wrongful convictions are at least due to some ethical violations on the part of attorneys, both prosecution

---

[120] *Id.* A famous example of this is *California v. Collins*, 68 Cal.2d 319, 438 P.2d 33 (1968). This case dealt with testimony about the probability that the perpetrators of the crime could have been someone other than the accused. It was ultimately determined that this expert testimony was based on unreliable mathematics and techniques.

[121] Raeder, *supra* note 32, at 1420.

[122] National Registry, *supra* note 48.

[123] Gross, *supra* note 39.

[124] *Id.*

[125] *Id.*

and defense alike. As Andrew Siegel has said, "Like an unhappy family, every wrongful conviction is unique."[126]

Prosecutorial misconduct is not a strange concept in the United States, often times being portrayed in various media. However, what is not widely known is exactly how much misconduct occurs with no punishment or discipline accompanying it. While the failure to punish those prosecuting attorneys who engage in misconduct is not a new concept or phenomenon,[127] it should definitely be alarming. There have been many cases throughout the country that illustrate the type of misconduct that prosecutors engage in, many of them leading to wrongful convictions.

For example, one prosecuting attorney served for over thirty years in Cleveland, Ohio before retiring in 2002.[128] During those thirty years that attorney prosecuted loads of cases and racked up a number of convictions, leading to his favorable reputation in the public's eye. However, six years after his retirement the attorney came to be known as representing the worst attributes of a prosecuting attorney.[129] Many of the convictions that he had acquired during his time as prosecuting attorney unraveled due to his misconduct.[130] This misconduct included failing to disclose key pieces of evidence to the accused before trial, allowing prosecution witnesses to lie at trial, and delivering improper and prejudicial closing arguments.[131]

---

[126] Andrew M. Siegel, *Moving Down the Wedge of Injustice: A Proposal for a Third Generation of Wrongful Conviction Scholarship and Advocacy*, 42 AM. CRIM. L.REV. 1219, 1223 (2005).

[127] Thomas P. Sullivan & Maurice Possley, *The Chronic Failure to Discipline Prosecutors for Misconduct: Proposals for Reform*, 105 J. CRIM. L. & CRIMINOLOGY 881, 884 (2015).

[128] Regina Brett, *County Prosecutor Bill Mason Should Retire Carmen Marino Award*, THE PLAIN DEALER BLOG (Oct. 3, 2008, 11:27 A.M.), http://wwwcleveland.com/brett/blog/index.ssf/2008/09/regina_brett_county_prosecutor.html

[129] *Id.*

[130] *Id.*

[131] Radley Balko, *Sorry About Your Time on Death Row, Pal, Nothing We Can Do*, WASHINGTON POST (Apr. 2, 2014), https://ww.washingtonpost.come/news/the-watch/wp/2014/04/02/sorry-about-your-time-on-death-row-pale-nothing-we-can-do/

However, despite the amount of misconduct that this attorney engaged in, the Ohio State Bar never publicly disciplined him.[132]

Ohio is definitely not alone in this behavior. An Arizona man who was convicted of resisting arrest and assaulting a police officer during the course of that arrest was exonerated after reports surfaced suggesting that the officers may have beaten the twenty-three-year-old man.[133] In California, two individuals had been convicted of a murder based on the identification from two witnesses.[134] Their convictions were overturned after one of the accused individuals discovered that the police had concealed evidence that one of the witnesses had recanted her statement and that law enforcement had paid the witnesses for their participation.[135]

Illinois also has a long and pitiful record in regards to prosecutorial misconduct.[136] For example, an individual accused of murder was convicted, in large part, due to one piece of evidence: a pair of shorts that were allegedly stained with blood consistent with the type of the eight-year-old victim.[137] Twelve years later the wrongfully accused individual was released when he showed that the stain was actually paint.[138] The prosecuting attorney in that case knew that the stain was not blood at the time of the trial.[139]

In 1992 four men were wrongfully accused of a double murder.[140] Their convictions were eventually overturned and vacated after the Attorney General's Office of Illinois learned of a handwritten note from a prosecuting attorney that showed that the police officers who had testified against one of the accused knew that the individual had been in jail at the

---

[132] The Supreme Court of Ohio, Office of Attorney Servs., Attorney Information (Carmen Michael Marino), http://www.supremecourtofohio.gov/AttySvcs/AttyReg/Public_AttorneyDetails.asp?ID=0001617

[133] Order Vacating Judgment and Convictions at 4-5, *Arizona v. Lewis*, CR20120036 (Ariz. Super. Ct. Dec. 3, 2013).

[134] Tennison v. San Francisco, 548 F.3d 1293, 1296, 1298 (9th Cir. 2008).

[135] *Id.*

[136] Sullivan & Possley, *supra* note 127, at 889.

[137] Illinois v. Miller, 148 N.E.2d 455, 458 (Ill. 1958).

[138] Miller v. Pate, 386 U.S. 1, 5 (1967).

[139] *Id.* at 6.

[140] Maurice Possley and Daniel Taylor, Univ. of Mich. Law Sch., Nat'l Registry of Exonerations, https://www.law.umich.edu/special/exoneration/Pages/casedetail.aspx?caseid=4212

time the murder occurred.[141] A man who was convicted three years later in 1995 and sentenced to fifty years was released after thirteen years.[142] In that case the state attorney's office knowingly withheld exculpatory evidence, thus violating *Brady*.[143]

Although it is difficult to find a case that addresses prosecutorial misconduct that does not explicitly deal with *Brady* violations, other aspects of prosecutorial misconduct are present in these cases, such as the Duke prosecutor who also engaged in wrongful pretrial publicity. While *Brady* violations are egregious in and of themselves, these other types of misconduct should be considered just as dangerous.

VI. Conclusion

Wrongful convictions have become a plague on our criminal justice system. Not only do they look bad upon prosecuting attorneys but they leave the general public with a sense of injustice. If the rising rate of exonerations and wrongful convictions was not enough to leave you suspended in disbelief, the fact that many of these instances could be completely prevented should.

Although prosecutorial misconduct is not happening in every single case, it does exist. The very existence of this type of behavior goes against the ideal of fairness in our criminal justice system that the Supreme Court has held so dear. Several of the Model Rules of Professional Conduct speak to the issues that have been addressed in this chapter. However, the rules are silent on the applicability to prosecutorial obligations in regards to witnesses who may be lying, such as jailhouse informants or dishonest experts. This gap leaves the prosecuting attorneys with complete discretion on the matter.

There has been an institutional and societal view that a prosecuting attorney's main goal is to gain convictions. This view has persisted despite the evidence that wrongful convictions have been occurring at an alarming rate. However, this is contrary to the role of prosecutors laid out in the rules and standards which describe prosecuting attorneys' duty is to be a seeker of justice, not just someone pushing for convictions.

---

[141] *Id.*

[142] Illinois v. Beaman, 890 N.E.2d 500, 502 (Ill. 2008).

[143] *Id.*

Wrongful convictions have been occurring at an alarming rate, and there are new exonerations seemingly every day. Since 1989 there have been 2,020 exonerations in the United States. While there are many contributing factors leading to these wrongful convictions and exonerations, one of the largest factors is "official misconduct."

Official Misconduct is a vast, undefined category. The main three types that were discussed in this chapter were *Brady* violations, jailhouse informants, and dishonest experts. All three of these categories come with their own dangers and contributions to wrongful convictions. The lack of regulations and rules governing the behavior of prosecuting attorneys does not help rein in the dangers associated with the use of jailhouse informants or dishonest experts, and despite the explicit ethics rule governing *Brady*, violations still occur. Without a change, or more accountability placed on prosecutors, who have a seemingly endless amount of discretion over their own work, this plague of wrongful convictions will continue to spread across our nation until it snuffs out our criminal justice system.

3

Attorney Sexual Misconduct: The ABA Update of Model Rule 8.4, the Addition to Model Rule 1.8, and the Consequences of Discrimination on Women in the Legal Profession

Sarah Cullum

I. Introduction

The American Bar Association (ABA) recently amended Model Rule of Professional Conduct (MRPC) 8.4: Misconduct to include an antidiscrimination provision. Attorneys are now expected to avoid engaging in discriminatory or harassing behavior, on the basis of "race, sex, religion, national origin, ethnicity, disability, age, sexual orientation, gender identity, marital status or socioeconomic status in conduct related to the practice of law."[1] The ABA made this change to protect the integrity of the legal profession. Certainly, the addition to Model Rule 8.4 holds attorneys accountable for unwelcome sexual conduct towards their colleagues by setting limits on what is appropriate behavior within the scope of the practice of law. These constraints are like those put in place by Model Rule 1.8, which deals with unethical client relationships. Like the antidiscrimination provision found in the new 2016 version of Rule 8.4, the provision in Rule 1.8 specifically forbidding sexual relationships between attorneys and their clients was added by the ABA in 2002.

This chapter will argue in four stages that while the ABA antidiscrimination update of Model Rule 8.4 is a significant step towards improving both sexual harassment problems and discrimination within the legal profession, this addition is simply the most recent to set specific restrictions on behavior. Attorney sexual misconduct is an institutional problem that needs greater ethical consideration to be fully eradicated. First, this chapter will address the legal history of sexual harassment in the United States, specifically through the lens of Title VII. Second, this chapter will examine the 2016 update of Model Rule of Professional

---

[1] AMERICAN BAR ASS'N, MODEL RULES OF PROF'L CONDUCT r. 8.4 (2016).

Conduct 8.4: Misconduct by exploring the ABA's motivations for change, the inclusion of antidiscrimination provisions in state ethics codes, and examples of discriminatory conduct in law firms throughout the United States. Third, this chapter will consider the 2002 addition to Model Rule of Professional Conduct 1.8: Current Clients: Specific Rules, which explicitly forbids sexual relationships between lawyers and their clients. Fourth, this chapter will consider the consequences of attorney sexual misconduct on women in the legal profession.

II. Legal History of Sexual Discrimination and Harassment in the United States

In order to understand the need for antidiscrimination rules in legal practice, it is important to examine the legal history of sexual harassment and discrimination in the United States. Since before the Civil War, scholars have addressed the nationwide epidemic of sexual harassment against women in the workplace.[2] Yet instead of actively working to correct this problem, Americans have often blamed women for their own sexual encounters.[3] At the turn of the twentieth century, few women "were willing to endure the damage to reputation and prospects for marriage that followed from bringing a rape complaint, and if they did, the prospects for vindication of their complaint were remote indeed."[4] These women faced an uphill battle since the legal standard in place at that time required that a woman claiming rape show both that the sexual contact was nonconsensual and that she was physically overpowered despite employing "utmost resistance."[5] While the women of the early American feminist and labor movements were unsuccessful in their attack on what is now defined as sexual harassment, they were nevertheless able to

---

[2] Reva B. Siegel, *A Short History of Sexual Harassment, Introduction to* DIRECTIONS IN SEXUAL HARASSMENT LAW 1, 3 (Catharine A. MacKinnon & Reva B. Siegel eds., Yale Univ. Press 2003).

[3] *Id.*

[4] *Id.* at 4.

[5] *Id.* ("In short, the law assumed that women in fact wanted the sexual advances and assaults that they claimed injured them. Unless women could show that they had performed an elaborate ritual of resistance, perfect compliance with the legally speci-fied terms of which was necessary to overcome the overwhelming presumption that women latently desired whatever was sexually done to them, they could expect little recourse from the criminal law.").

pinpoint and raise awareness of the issues that eventually formed the platforms of the modern feminist and labor movements.[6]

In 1986, in *Meritor Savings Bank, FSB v. Vinson*, the United States Supreme Court held that sexual harassment that leads to a "hostile or abusive work environment" is a form of sex discrimination under Title VII of the Civil Rights Act of 1964.[7] In that case, the former employee of a bank, claimed that she had been sexually harassed by her supervisor during the course of her employment.[8] The Court stated that when a supervisor sexually harasses a subordinate employee based on that employee's sex, the supervisor is engaging in discrimination "on the basis of sex."[9] The Court understood that sexual harassment "on the basis of sex" impedes sexual equality in the workplace, much like racial harassment results in racial inequality.[10]

Expanding on its decision in *Vinson*, in 1993 the Supreme Court, in *Harris v. Forklift Systems, Inc.*, held that harassment can constitute an "abusive work environment" even if the behavior does not "seriously affect psychological well-being" of an employee or lead an employee to "suffer injury."[11] In *Harris*, a woman sued her former employer, claiming that the president of the company affronted the woman because of her gender and often made her the subject of sexual anecdotes.[12] The Court reaffirmed the *Vinson* standard, stating that Title VII is violated when discriminatory conduct in a professional setting is persistent enough to generate a "hostile or abusive" environment.[13] The Court then clarified

---

[6] *Id.* at 8.

[7] Meritor Savings Bank, FSB v. Vinson, 477 U.S. 57, 66 (1986).

[8] *Id.* at 60.

[9] *Id.* at 64.

[10] *Id.* at 67 ("Sexual harassment which creates a hostile or offensive environment for members of one sex is every bit the arbitrary barrier to sexual equality at the workplace that racial harassment is to racial equality. Surely, a requirement that a man or woman run a gauntlet of sexual abuse in return for the privilege of being allowed to work and make a living can be as demeaning and disconcerting as the harshest racial epithets.").

[11] Harris v. Forklift Systems, Inc., 510 U.S. 17, 21-23 (1993).

[12] *Id.* at 19.

[13] *Id.* at 21-22 (quoting *Vinson*, 477 U.S. at 64, 67) ("As we pointed out in *Vinson*, 'mere utterance of an . . . epithet which engenders offensive feelings in an employee,' does not sufficiently affect the conditions of employment to implicate Title VII. Conduct that is not severe or pervasive enough to create an objectively hostile or abusive work environment—an environment that a reasonable person would find hostile or abu-

that standard, explaining that a workplace environment can only be considered "hostile or abusive" after all the circumstances have been examined.[14] This inquiry can include the regularity of the behavior, its harshness, whether it physically threatens or humiliates, and whether it obstructs the ability of the employee to accomplish work.[15] Finally, the Court held that while the effect on an employee's psychological well-being is important in deciding if the employee actually found the workplace offensive, psychological harm is not dispositive and must be weighed among other related factors.[16]

Five years later, in *Oncale v. Sundowner Offshore Services*, the Court held that Title VII did not exclude discrimination claims "on the basis of sex" where plaintiff and defendant were the same gender.[17] In that case, a man working offshore on an oil platform claimed he was subjected to sexually demeaning conduct by other male members of the crew, was sexually assaulted by two male crew members, and was also threatened with rape by a male crew member.[18] The Court found that discriminatory actions do not have to be driven by sexual desire to qualify as discrimination "on the basis of sex."[19] Further, the Court stated that the plaintiff must always support a showing that the questioned behavior was not simply touched with sexually offensive remarks, but was founded in "discrimination . . . because of . . . sex."[20] Finally, the Court admonished "that courts and juries do not mistake ordinary socializing in the workplace—such as male-on-male horseplay or intersexual flirtation—for discriminatory 'conditions of employment.'"[21]

Certainly both *Vinson* and *Harris* describe the "classic harassment scenario," or the idea that a female employee is required to take part in

---

sive—is beyond Title VII's purview. Likewise, if the victim does not subjectively perceive the environment to be abusive, the conduct has not actually altered the conditions of the victim's employment, and there is no Title VII violation.").

[14] *Harris*, 510 U.S. at 22.

[15] *Id.*

[16] *Id.* at 23.

[17] Oncale v. Sundowner Offshore Servs., 523 U.S. 75, 82 (1998).

[18] *Id.* at 77.

[19] *Id.* at 80.

[20] *Id.* at 81.

[21] *Id.* (citing *Harris*, 510 U.S. at 21) (citing *Vinson*, 477 U.S. at 67).

unwanted sexual relations to remain employed.[22] This sexually coercive behavior creates stereotypical circumstances which allow for the perpetuation of traditional gender stereotypes in the workplace.[23] Although *Oncale* involved a dispute between men, that case and situations like it involve many of the same basic issues as *Vinson* and *Harris*: examples of masculine sexual aggression employed to intimidate and maintain a patriarchal social order within the workplace.

III. Model Rule of Professional Conduct 8.4: Misconduct

A. American Bar Association Update

Prior to the official change by the ABA in 2016, Model Rule of Professional Conduct 8.4: Misconduct stated:

It is professional misconduct for a lawyer to:

(a) violate or attempt to violate the Rules of Professional Conduct, knowingly assist or induce another to do so, or do so through the acts of another;

(b) commit a criminal act that reflects adversely on the lawyer's honesty, trustworthiness or fitness as a lawyer in other respects;

(c) engage in conduct involving dishonesty, fraud, deceit or misrepresentation;

(d) engage in conduct that is prejudicial to the administration of justice;

(e) state or imply an ability to influence improperly a government agency or official or to achieve results by means that violate the Rules of Professional Conduct or other law; or

---

[22] Reva B. Siegel, *A Short History of Sexual Harassment, Introduction to* Directions in Sexual Harassment Law 1, 22 (Catharine A. MacKinnon & Reva B. Siegel eds., Yale Press 2003).

[23] *Id.* ("Men are not using economic power to secure sexual access to women they otherwise would not have; rather . . . men use sexualized and nonsexualized conduct to communicate to women their outsider status in the workplace . . . . Harm occurs—not through the traditional pathway in which the harassed woman lacks capacity to refuse an unwanted sexual relationship—but instead because the harasser uses sexualized and nonsexualized conduct to construct the harassed woman as an outsider in the workplace—de-authorized and denigrated, in her own eyes and in the eyes of others.").

(f) knowingly assist a judge or judicial officer in conduct that is a violation of applicable rules of judicial conduct or other law.[24]

Although not explicitly stated in this version of Rule 8.4, Comment 3[25] to the rule included an antidiscrimination provision.[26] However, Comments do not have the same authority as Rules and therefore can only serve as guidance.[27] Indeed, while Comment 3 contained an antidiscrimination provision, practitioners expressed a need for a guiding rule that would be enforceable during disciplinary proceedings concerning harassment or discrimination.[28] Thus, on August 8, 2016, the ABA amended Model Rule 8.4 by adding paragraph (g),[29] prohibiting lawyers from:

(g) engag[ing] in conduct that the lawyer knows or reasonably should know is harassment or discrimination on the base of race, sex, religion, national origin, ethnicity, disability, age, sexual orientation, gender identity, marital status or socioeconomic status in conduct related to the practice of law. This paragraph does not limit the ability of a lawyer to accept, decline or withdraw from a representation in accordance with Rule

---

24 AMERICAN BAR ASS'N, MODEL RULES OF PROF'L CONDUCT r. 8.4 (2015).

25 AMERICAN BAR ASS'N, MODEL RULES OF PROF'L CONDUCT r. 8.4 cmt. 3 (2015) ("A lawyer who, in the course of representing a client, knowingly manifests by words or conduct, bias or prejudice based upon race, sex, religion, national origin, disability, age, sexual orientation or socioeconomic status, violates paragraph (d) when such actions are prejudicial to the administration of justice.").

26 Hon. Louraine C. Arkfeld, *Amending Rule 8.4 of the Model Rules of Professional Conduct*, 1.7 Voice of Experience (ABA Senior Lawyers Division, Chi., Ill.), July 2016.

27 *Id.* (citing AM. BAR ASS'N, MODEL RULES OF PROF'L CONDUCT Preamble and Scope (2016)) ("Comments do not add obligations to the Rules but provide guidance for practicing in compliance with the Rules. . . . The Comments are intended as guides to interpretation, but the test of each Rule is authoritative.").

28 Peter Geraghty, *ABA Adopts New Anti-Discrimination Rule 8.4(g)*, Eye on Ethics (ETHICSearch/ABA Center for Professional Responsibility, Chi., Ill.), Sept. 2016 (quoting AM. BAR ASS'N, MODEL RULES OF PROF'L CONDUCT r. 8.4 cmt. (2016) ("[3] A lawyer who, in the course of representing a client, knowingly manifests by words or conduct, bias or prejudice based upon race, sex, religion, national origin, disability, age, sexual orientation or socioeconomic status, violates paragraph (d) when such actions are prejudicial to the administration of justice. Legitimate advocacy respecting the foregoing factors does not violate paragraph (d). A trial judge's finding that peremptory challenges were exercised on a discriminatory basis does not alone establish a violation of this rule.").

29 American Bar Ass'n, "Model Rule of Professional Conduct 8.4, Revised Resolution 109 Adopted by ABA HOD," http://www.americanbar.org/groups/professional _responsibility/committees_commissions/ethicsandprofessionalresponsibility/modru leprofconduct8_4.html (last visited Mar. 21, 2017).

1.16. This paragraph does not preclude legitimate advice or ad-vocacy consistent with these Rules.[30]

This addition makes it misconduct to participate in discrimination or harassment associated with the practice of law.[31] In other words, it "treats as harassment any demeaning verbal or physical conduct or unwanted verbal or physical sexual conduct, by a lawyer when such conduct occurs in relation to the practice of law. Conduct related to the practice of law includes activities such as law firm dinners and events at which the lawyers were present because of their association with the law firm."[32]

Both the reasonableness and knowledge requirements included in new paragraph (g) of Rule 8.4 protect lawyers from being prosecuted based on conduct that they did not know was harassment or discrimination and defend against conduct that a reasonable lawyer should have known was harassment or discrimination.[33] Certainly, the ABA also adopted paragraphs three through five of the Comment to 8.4,[34] in order to further guide the interpretation of the change to Rule 8.4.[35] This includes defining discrimination and harassment in Comment 3 and defining "conduct related to the practice of law" in Comment 4.[36] Discrimination involves prejudicial verbal or physical conduct, specifically

---

[30] AMERICAN BAR ASS'N, MODEL RULES OF PROF'L CONDUCT r. 8.4 (2017).

[31] Arkfield, 1.7 Voice of Experience (2016).

[32] *Id.*

[33] Geraghty, Eye on Ethics (2016).

[34] *Id.*

[35] AMERICAN BAR ASS'N, MODEL RULES OF PROF'L CONDUCT r. 8.4 cmt. (2017).

[36] *Id.* ("[3] Discrimination and harassment by lawyers in violation of paragraph (g) undermine confidence in the legal profession and the legal system. Such discrimination includes harmful verbal or physical conduct that manifests bias or prejudice towards others. Harassment includes sexual harassment and derogatory or demeaning verbal or physical conduct. Sexual harassment includes unwelcome sexual advances, requests for sexual favors, and other unwelcome verbal or physical conduct of a sexual nature. The substantive law of antidiscrimination and anti-harassment statutes and case law may guide application of paragraph (g). [4] Conduct related to the practice of law includes representing clients; interacting with witnesses, coworkers, court personnel, lawyers and others while engaged in the practice of law; operating or managing a law firm or law practice; and participating in bar association, business or social activities in connection with the practice of law. Lawyers may engage in conduct undertaken to promote diversity and inclusion without violating this Rule by, for example, implementing initiatives aimed at recruiting, hiring, retaining and advancing diverse employees or sponsoring diverse law student organizations.").

unwanted sexual advances, requests for sexual favors, or any other unwelcome sexual behavior.[37] Past ABA President, Paulette Brown, explained the importance of continuing to update the Model Rules, stating:

> The current Model Rules of Professional Conduct, however, do not yet reflect the monumental achievements that have been accomplished to protect clients and the public against harassment and intimidation. The association should now correct this omission. It is in the public's interest. It is in the profession's interest. It makes it clear that discrimination, harassment, bias and prejudice do not belong in conduct related to the practice of law.[38]

Despite the support garnered by the antidiscrimination provision, some expressed concern that false complaints would be filed to gain a lead in a matter.[39] Some also argued that the antidiscrimination provision would empower those in state bar associations to punish attorneys with more conservative values.[40] These critics hold the belief that the new antidiscrimination provision is proof that "the ABA is totally uninterested in professional ethics based on sound moral choices, and has shifted its agenda to imposing a progressive political orthodoxy upon the legal profession, through the politicization of legal ethics."[41] However, prior to the official update twenty-three states had adopted an antidiscrimination or anti-harassment provision into their ethics rules.[42] Contrary to the

---

37 *Id.*

38 *Quoted in* Geraghty, Eye on Ethics (2016).

39 *See* Arkfield, 1.7 Voice of Experience (2016).

40 Herbert W. Titus and William J. Olson, *The ABA's Plan to Impose Political Correctness on the Practice of Law*, AMERICAN THINKER, http://www.american thinker.com/articles/2016/08/the_abas_plan_to_impose_political_ correctness_on _the_practice_of_law.html (last visited Mar. 21, 2017) ("But it has long been recognized that the equality principle that applies to race does not apply to other types of classifications, even including sex. If there can be men's and women's basketball, volleyball, and track teams, why can there not be law firms which limit their practice to only wives or only husbands in family law matters? Why should such firms be outlawed because they make a distinction between clients on the basis of their 'marital status'? What about a person's 'sexual orientation'? Or their 'gender identity'? Neither of these latter two terms is objectively determinable or even objectively observable. Rather, they are completely subjective, dependent solely on a person's self-perception. Surely lawyers—of all people—ought to know better than to concoct such a vague and standardless rule.").

41 *Id.*

42 Arkfield, 1.7 Voice of Experience (2016).

fears of critics, the experience in these jurisdictions has been that where an antidiscrimination or antiharassment provisions are in place, false complaints against attorneys are not actually filed. Rather, the result of the statute is that based on ethical grounds now attorneys engaging in discriminatory conduct can face legal consequences.[43]

There are a wide range of interpretations among the states of the addition to Model Rule 8.4(g).[44] As of September 15, 2016, only twelve states have not adopted any version of Model Rule 8.4 (g).[45] While the exact language of Model Rule 8.4 (g) is not used in any state rule, many states have implemented provisions with the same connotation.[46] However, these inclusions vary drastically by state.[47] Some states have incorporated a more concise version of Model Rule 8.4 (g) than that adopted by the ABA. For example, the Alabama rule avers that attorneys may not "engage in any other conduct that adversely reflects on his fitness to practice law.[48] Succinct rules like this one do not provide enough information for attorneys about bigoted actions and therefore are unlikely to prevent harassment from occurring.[49] Discrimination is able to be addressed more fully in jurisdictions where the rule is specific in guiding conduct.[50] For example, the New York rule is an expanded version of Model Rule 8.4(g) and states that:

[A lawyer or law firm shall not]

---

[43] *Id.* While victims of sexual discrimination have always been able to file civil and criminal charges against their abusers, the update of Model Rule 8.4 is the first explicitly forbidding discrimination within the scope of the practice of law. Therefore, the provision is the first to allow claims against attorneys on ethical grounds.

[44] AMERICAN BAR ASS'N, MODEL RULES OF PROF'L CONDUCT r. 8.4 advisory committee's note (2016) (Variations of the ABA Model Rules of Professional Conduct).

[45] *Id.* These twelve states have not adopted any version of Model Rule 8.4 (g): Arizona, Arkansas, Connecticut, Idaho, Mississippi, Montana, Nevada, Oklahoma, Pennsylvania, South Dakota, Utah, and West Virginia.

[46] *Id.*

[47] *Id.*

[48] *Id.* The rule in Kansas is almost identical and expects those in the legal profession should not "engage in any other conduct that adversely reflects on the lawyer's fitness to practice law." Massachusetts is also similar and states that attorneys should not "engage in any other conduct that adversely reflects on his or her fitness to practice law."

[49] *Id.*

[50] *Id.*

(g) [u]nlawfully discriminate in the practice of law, including in hiring, promoting, or otherwise determining conditions of employment on the basis of age, race, creed, color, national origin, sex, disability, marital status or sexual orientation. Where there is a tribunal with jurisdiction to hear a complaint, if timely brought, other than a Department Disciplinary Committee, a complaint based on unlawful discrimination shall be brought before such tribunal in the first instance. A certified copy of a determination by such a tribunal, which has become final and enforceable and as to which the right to judicial or appellate review has been exhausted, finding that the lawyer has engaged in an unlawful discriminatory practice shall constitute prima facie evidence of professional misconduct in a disciplinary proceeding; or

(h) Engage in any other conduct that adversely reflects on the lawyer's fitness as a lawyer.[51]

Indeed, this adaptation not only prohibits prejudicial behavior, but also standardizes the procedure of bringing a complaint.[52] Comprehensive rules set unambiguous boundaries on what is considered misconduct.

B. Sexual Discrimination in U.S. Law Firms

Sexual discrimination and harassment are major problems in U.S. law firms.[53] Typically these incidents occur between more senior male employees and subordinate female employees. For example, in one case concerning the world's largest law firm of Baker & McKenzie, one male lawyer, Mr. Greenstein, forced himself on several subordinate female employees with inappropriate remarks and fondling.[54] One of Greenstein's secretaries, Ms. Weeks, accounted that Greenstein "grabbed her breast while dropping M&M candies in the pocket of her blouse. Then he held her arms behind her back, thrust her chest forward and demanded to

---

[51] *Id.* States with similar rules to New York that include information about procedure include: Florida, Georgia, Illinois, Texas, Washington, and Wyoming. Florida and Georgia have the most comprehensive understandings of Model Rule 8.4 (g) with their versions of the rule containing the most details.

[52] *Id.*

[53] Jane Gross, *When the Biggest Firm Faces Sexual Harassment Suit*, NEW YORK TIMES, (July 29, 1994), http://www.nytimes.com/1994/07/29/us/when-the-biggest-firm-faces-sexual-harassment-suit.html?pagewanted=all (last visited Mar. 21, 2017).

[54] *Id.*

know which of her breasts was larger." While Greenstein denied these claims and other accusations, Ms. Weeks's lawyer told the *New York Times* that Greenstein had harassed a minimum of ten women in over six years with Baker & McKenzie.[55] However, the firm tolerated and even covered up Greenstein's misconduct because of the narrow definition of sexual harassment and the tendency of firms to suppress women's grievances about inappropriate remarks and actions.[56]

In another example, a New York federal jury found that the firm Faruqi & Faruqi and its partner, Juan Monteverde, were accountable in the creation of a "hostile work environment."[57] The jury awarded former Faruqi associate, Alexandra Marchuk, $140,000 in damages.[58] Marchuk claimed that Monteverde kissed her and grabbed her chest without her consent, outside of a bar in Manhattan. She also asserted that "he made sexually charged comments and vulgar jokes in the presence of co-workers and that he sexually assaulted her after a drunken holiday party."[59] In a similar situation, Elizabeth Bailey, a former associate at Nelson, Levine, DeLuca & Hamilton LLC sued over what she described as "frat house culture" at the firm.[60] Bailey averred that she and several other female associates were asked to pose for a pin-up calendar.[61] Indeed, sexual harassment is a major problem, even in legal workplaces, because many firms still lack effective policies to deal with such behavior.[62]

Furthermore, many first-hand accounts exist of women's experiences with discrimination in the legal profession.[63] These narratives relay the graphic experiences that many women are subjected to within the legal

---

[55] *Id.*

[56] *Id.*

[57] Beth Winegarner, *After Faruqi, More Female Attys to Sue for Sex Harassment,* LAW 360 (Apr. 21, 2015, 5:58 PM), https://www.law360.com/articles/644709/after-faruqi-more-female-attys-to-sue-for-sex-harassment (last visited Mar. 21, 2017).

[58] *Id.*

[59] *Id.*

[60] *Id.*

[61] *Id.*

[62] *Id.*

[63] Staci Zaretsky, *The Pink Ghetto: Shocking Stories About Sexual Harassment at Law Firms,* ABOVE THE LAW (Jan. 6, 2016, 11:59 AM), http://abovethelaw.com/2016/01/the-pink-ghetto-shocking-stories-about-sexual-harassment-at-law-firms/?rf=1

profession. Many male attorneys in senior positions abuse their power by sexually harassing women in subordinate positions and these accounts demonstrate the need for the recent revision of Model Rule 8.4 to include an antidiscrimination provision. While sexual harassment of course has the possibility of occurring between people of any gender, most of the available stories seem to involve a male discriminating against a female colleague.

One woman illustrates her experience with a younger partner at her firm who would give "impromptu back rubs, foot rubs, or hand rubs."[64] The partner would also make sexual statements to coworkers "about putting a female associate in a thong for the firm's next ad or telling an associate who had put on stress weight that she must be good at blow-jobs or her boyfriend would have left her by now."[65] This same partner would occasionally follow younger associates out after work, proceeding to drunkenly grind against them and touch them in other unacceptable ways. Another woman describes a male partner in her firm approaching her after a case by stating the "[he] would love to clean [her] drawers" and asking her if she needed assistance.[66] The same man requested that the associate wear stilettos everyday and also placed his hand on her knee at a work event.[67] The same woman was also told that she was not partner material because the partner believed that blonde haired women could not be taken seriously because they were "too tempting and unprofessional."[68] The woman asked for substantive reasons as to why she did not qualify for partner and was told that she would not be supported when her name came up.[69]

An additional woman describes her being harassed by a male partner, stating:

> [She] was sitting in a meeting with several male partners and a male associate. [She] didn't know any of them; [she] was new to the case team. In the middle of the meeting, one of the partners got up from his chair, walked over to where [she] was sitting,

---

[64] *Id.*

[65] *Id.*

[66] *Id.*

[67] *Id.*

[68] *Id.*

[69] *Id.*

pressed against the back of [her] chair so [she] couldn't push back from the table, and started rubbing [her] shoulders. [She] was so utterly shocked [she] didn't know what to do. [She] tried to shrug him off and push him away, to no avail. [She] didn't want to make a scene since [she] was new to the team. No one else said a word. Eventually he went back to his seat. After the meeting, the male associate commented that [she] must be close to that partner. [She] said [she] didn't know him. The partner started leaving [her] voicemails about how much he missed me and wanted to see me. [She] called the head partner on the case and said [she] couldn't work under these conditions. He said, "It seems to me women have all sorts of ways of telling men they're not interested. If he's not getting the message, you must be sending the wrong message." The employment lawyers caught wind of [her] complaint but [she] refused to elaborate, figuring it would be career suicide. A week later, [she] was told [she] was being taken off partnership track; without explanation.[70]

Another female associate describes being taken to lunch and mentored by the oldest partner at her firm.[71] While it seemed friendly at first, the partner stopped by her office with earrings as a gift "because he noticed that [she] always wore 'exotic' earrings."[72] The associate expressed feeling embarrassed, but thanked the partner to avoid an uncomfortable situation.[73] Since she had recently graduated from law school she was afraid that her job and reputation would be negatively affected by speaking with Human Resources.[74] The woman asserted that the partner continued to give her jewelry throughout her first year at the firm.[75] When the associate got married, she requested that the partner stop giving her jewelry and stated that "[she] was not comfortable accepting jewelry from a man who was not [her] husband."[76] The partner resisted and questioned whether it was the associate or her husband who was uncomfortable.

---

[70] *Id.*

[71] *Id.*

[72] *Id.*

[73] *Id.*

[74] *Id.*

[75] *Id.*

[76] *Id.*

When the female associate continued to refuse the gift, the male partner responded with "you know that you're not the only one I give jewelry to."[77]

The update to Rule 8.4 protects attorneys from sexual discrimination in the workplace, helping to alleviate many of the fears experienced by women in workplace harassment situations. Sexual misconduct must be eliminated from the legal profession for the purposes of impartiality and fairness.

IV. Model Rule of Professional Conduct 1.8 Conflict of Interest: Current Clients: Specific Rules

A. American Bar Association 2002 Update

In 2002 the ABA added paragraph (j) to Model Rule of Professional Conduct 1.8 Conflict of Interest: Current Clients: Specific Rules.[78] This provision states that "[a] lawyer shall not have sexual relations with a client unless a consensual sexual relationship existed between them when the client-lawyer relationship commenced."[79] The addition was made after a number of states made adaptations to their rules unambiguously controlling sexual conduct between lawyers and their clients.[80] The ABA reasoned that while most abhorrent attorney conduct was attended to in other rules, the rules were not sufficient in dealing with client-lawyer sexual misconduct.[81] The ABA believed that both attorneys and their clients would be protected by this specific rule—not only because the rule warns lawyers of the hazards of a sexual relationship with a client, but also because it warns clients that a lawyer possibly "violated ethical obligations" by participating in such conduct.[82]

Indeed, in Comment 17 of Rule 1.8 the ABA extrapolates that client-lawyer romantic relationships are problematic because of their fiduciary

---

[77] *Id.*

[78] Dane S. Ciolino, *Rule 1.8. Conflict of Interest: Current Clients—Specific Rules*, Louisiana Legal Ethics (Jan. 18, 2017), https://lalegalethics.org/louisiana-rules-of-professional-conduct/article-1-client-lawyer-relationship/rule-1-8-conflict-of-interest-current-clients-specific-rules/#Paragraph-j-Sex-With-Clients

[79] AMERICAN BAR ASS'N, MODEL RULES OF PROF'L CONDUCT r. 1.8 (2015).

[80] Ciolino, Louisiana Legal Ethics (2017).

[81] *Id.*

[82] *Id.*

nature.[83] Because of the emotions involved, these types of relationships could lead to abuse of the attorney's position as trustee.[84] The attorney unfairly holds a position of power over the client.[85] The inequality in the relationship disadvantages the client since it prejudices the lawyer's ability to remain impartial in their professional decisions.[86] "Such an unequal relationship, where the client in most cases is emotionally and financially vulnerable, is a recipe for abuse by attorneys.[87]

These dangers led the ABA to adopt a total ban on client-lawyer relationships.[88] The ABA judged that a partial ban, only prohibiting these relationships when duress or incompetence was involved, would not realistically address the dilemma of conflict of interest.[89] However, the ABA included a provision allowing for romantic relationships that existed before the establishment of the client-lawyer relationship, citing that these relationships do not create a conflict of interest because they do not involve coercion.[90] Comment 18 of Rule 1.8 clarifies that although these pre-existing relationships have less possibility for exploitation, the

---

[83] AMERICAN BAR ASS'N, MODEL RULES OF PROF'L CONDUCT r. 1.8 cmt. 17 (2015) ("The relationship between lawyer and client is a fiduciary one in which the lawyer occupies the highest position of trust and confidence. The relationship is almost always unequal; thus, a sexual relationship between lawyer and client can involve unfair exploitation of the lawyer's fiduciary role, in violation of the lawyer's basic ethical obligation not to use the trust of the client to the client's disadvantage. In addition, such a relationship presents a significant danger that, because of the lawyer's emotional involvement, the lawyer will be unable to represent the client without impairment of the exercise of independent professional judgment. Moreover, a blurred line between the professional and personal relationships may make it difficult to predict to what extent client confidences are protected by privilege only when they are imparted in the context of the client-lawyer relationship. Because of the significant danger of harm to clients interests and because the client's own emotional involvement renders it unlikely that the client could give adequate informed consent, this Rule prohibits the lawyer from having sexual relations with a client regardless of whether the relationship is consensual and regardless of the absence of prejudice to the client.").

[84] *Id.*

[85] Abed Awad, *Attorney-Client Sexual Relations*, 22 J. LEGAL PROF. 131, 131-32 (1998).

[86] AMERICAN BAR ASS'N, MODEL RULES OF PROF'L CONDUCT r. 1.8 cmt. 17 (2015).

[87] Awad, 22 J. LEGAL PROF. at 132.

[88] Ciolino, Louisiana Legal Ethics (2017).

[89] *Id.*

[90] *Id.*

attorney should consider whether the relationship would hinder their ability to effectively represent the client.[91]

B. Attorney-Client Sexual Misconduct Case Law

Prior to the official adaptation of Rule 1.8 by the ABA in 2002 by new paragraph (j), several states examined the ethical quandary of sexual relationships between attorneys and their clients. In *In re Discipline of Heard*, the Supreme Court of Washington upheld a disciplinary board's recommended sanction to suspend an attorney's license to practice law for two years.[92] In that case, an attorney representing a woman in a personal injury action participated in consensual sexual relations with his client after the two "discussed the case" over drinks.[93] The attorney was fully aware of the vulnerability of his client, having access to her medical history and the knowledge that she had a history of drug and alcohol abuse.[94] Further, the attorney resolved to keep $50,000 cash for his fee without his client consenting to the arrangement and without providing her with an account of the settlement proceedings.[95] The court held that the attorney put his own interests before those of his client in his handling of the settlement.[96] Although Washington had yet to adopt an explicit rule forbidding sexual attorney-client relationships, the court reasoned that sexual relations with a client can establish "moral turpitude" and the justification to levy sanctions.[97] In this case, the attorney's use of his profession to sexually exploit a vulnerable client indeed "constituted

---

[91] AMERICAN BAR ASS'N, MODEL RULES OF PROF'L CONDUCT r. 1.8 cmt. 18 (2015) ("[18] Sexual relationships that predate the client-lawyer relationship are not prohibited. Issues relating to the exploitation of the fiduciary relationship and client dependency are diminished when the sexual relationship existed prior to the commencement of the client-lawyer relationship. However, before proceeding with the representation in these circumstances, the lawyer should consider whether the lawyer's ability to represent the client will be materially limited by the relationship.").

[92] *In re* Discipline of Heard, 136 Wn.2d 405, 409 (1998).

[93] *Id.* at 412.

[94] *Id.* at 411.

[95] *Id.* at 412.

[96] *Id.* at 417.

[97] *Id.* at 419.

moral turpitude."[98] The attorney was suspended from the practice of law for two years and forced to pay restitution in the amount of $28,334.34 plus interest.[99]

In *In re Berg*, the Supreme Court of Kansas held that an attorney should be disbarred after having inappropriate sexual encounters with several of his clients who were going through divorce proceedings.[100] The court reasoned that this conduct constituted the attorney using "his license to practice law to the disadvantage of his clients."[101] Similarly, in *In re Ashe*, the Supreme Court of Louisiana suspended an attorney from the practice of law for two years, where the attorney sexually exploited a client.[102] In that case, an attorney told his client that he would not adequately represent her, unless she responded to his sexual advances.[103] The court inferred that by attempting to participate in a sexual relationship with his client, the attorney failed to exercise independent judgment.[104] Furthermore, the court found the attorney's "conduct here to be 'sexual exploitation of a nature that indicates he is unworthy of the confidence reposed in him.'"[105]

Certainly, it is with similar logic to the previous cases that the ABA adapted Model Rule 1.8(j), and states have used this rule as a model for their own ethics codes. In *Attorney Grievance Commission of Maryland v. Allan J. Culver, Jr.*, the Court of Appeals of Maryland ordered an attorney disbarred where the attorney participated in inappropriate sexual intercourse with his client.[106] In that case the attorney "made threats that if [his client] did not cooperate with him and accede to his

---

98 *Id.* at 422-23; *cf. In re* Discipline of Halverson, 140 Wn.2d 475 (2000) ("The Board properly found that under the circumstances Halverson's affair with Wickersham did not constitute moral turpitude.").

99 *In re Discipline of Heard*, 136 Wn. at 425.

100 *In re* Berg, 264 Kan. 254, 281 (1998).

101 *Id.*

102 *In re* Ashy, 721 So.2d 859, 868 (La. 1998). *See also In re* DeFrancesch, 877 So.2d 71 (La. 2004), in which an attorney was suspended for two years where his sexual misconduct with a client was deemed to violate various Louisiana Rules of Professional Conduct.

103 *In re Ashy*, 721 So.2d at 861.

104 *Id.* at 867.

105 *Id.* at 868.

106 Attorney Griev. Comm'n v. Culver, 381 Md. 241, 249 (2004).

sexual demands, he would deliberately sabotage her case so that she would lose custody of her children."[107] Because the client was emotionally susceptible at the time of the sexual contact, the attorney retained excessive influence over his client and took advantage of her exposure by engaging in sex acts.[108] The court reasoned that the attorney violated the Maryland Rules of Professional Conduct by allowing his personal interests to obstruct the representation of his client.[109]

In *Cleveland Metropolitan Bar Association v. Lockshin*, an attorney was suspended indefinitely from practicing law where he violated the Ohio Code of Professional Responsibility by engaging in improper sexual communications with clients, a law enforcement officer, and a potential witness.[110] The court in that case argued that the attorney's behavior had a negative impact on his clients, many of whom were young and defenseless women.[111] The attorney's conduct "reveals respondent's selfish motive to advance his own sexual interests at his clients' expense."[112]

Overall, these examples of attorney-client sexual misconduct demonstrate the scope of the problem of sexual harassment and encourage the continued modification of ethics rules to protect both lawyers and their clients.

---

[107] *Id.* at 257.

[108] *Id.* ("Ms. [the client] was emotionally upset and vulnerable at that time due to her pending divorce and her husband's threats to take the children away from her, as well as financial pressure resulting from the divorce and litigation expenses. [Attorney], while maintaining a confidential relationship with Ms. [the client], exercised a degree of undue influence over and took advantage of her vulnerability, such as convincing her to perform fellatio on him on two occasions.").

[109] *Id.* at 261-62 ("Respondent placed his interests in continuing to be paid for his representation above Ms. [the client]'s interests when he advised her to obtain cash advances on credit cards to pay her fee with the intent to have the credit card debt discharged in bankruptcy. Respondent placed his personal interests above those of Ms. [the client] perform other sex acts. Ms. [the client] was in an unstable emotional state due to her pending divorce litigation and Respondent took advantage of her situation for his own personal interest.").

[110] Cleveland Metro. Bar Ass'n v. Lockshin, 125 Ohio St. 3d 529, 529-30 (2010).

[111] *Id.* at 538.

[112] *Id.*

V. Consequences of Sexual Misconduct in the Legal Profession

Although years apart, the ABA updates of Model Rules 1.8 and 8.4 both occurred after multiple state jurisdictions adopted rules against attorney-client relationships and discrimination, respectively. These additions encourage attorneys to make ethical choices regarding sex by outlining behaviors to avoid. Typically, in cases concerning discrimination, sexuality is used to either determine who is protected under the law or explain sexual behavior.[113] "Title VII prohibits discrimination 'because of sex' rather than discrimination 'by sexual means.'"[114] In these types of cases, causation is determined by examining "whether the harm to the plaintiff was discriminatory in nature."[115] Although discrimination because of sex violates Title VII, the ABA provided no ethical protections for attorneys as victims of sexual misconduct prior to the 2016 update of Model Rule 8.4. The recent update provides guidance for classifying discrimination and warns attorneys of misbehavior. However, the claims being filed by women against their male colleagues suggests that the Model Rules of Professional Conduct need further adaptation to completely eradicate inequality and sexism in the legal profession.

Legal scholars argue that sexual harassment violates formal equality principles because it causes women to be constrained in a way that men are not.[116] Formal equality contends that heterosexual desire is targeted at the opposite sex and therefore sexual advances made by a male, establish that a woman's sex is the 'but for cause' of harassment.[117] Others believe that this theory simply reinforces ideas about traditional gender roles and "that sex discrimination law has committed a fundamental error by

---

[113] David S. Schwartz, *When is Sex Because of Sex? The Causation Problem in Sexual Harassment Law*, 150 U. PA. L. REV. 1697, 1706 (2002) ("'[S]ex' should properly refer to the two biological sex categories typically assigned at birth based on anatomical and physiological distinctions, and . . . 'gender' should mean the social and cultural understandings derived from sex. 'Sexual orientation' refers to the human inclination 'toward affectional intimacy with members of one particular sex or of both sexes.' By 'sexual behavior' or 'sexual conduct' . . . physical sexual acts or communicative acts depicting sexual acts. 'Sexuality' is a blanket term that includes both sexual orientation and behavior.").

[114] *Id.* at 1708.

[115] *Id.* at 1710.

[116] *Id.* at 1752.

[117] *Id.* at 1753.

assuming the existence of two immutable biological sexes, each of which carries an inextricable gender."[118] When gender is separated from sex, it becomes clear that biological sex is less to blame for incidents of discrimination than hetero-masculine gender expectations.[119]

One scholar discusses the problems of traditional gender stereotyping, stating:

> [T]he sexual harassment of a woman by a man is an instance of sexism precisely because the act embodies fundamental gender stereotypes: men as sexual conquerors and women as sexually conquered, men as masculine sexual subjects and women as feminine sexual objects. . . . Sexual harassment is a technology of sexism. It is a disciplinary practice that inscribes, enforces, and polices the identities of both harasser and victim according to a system of gender norms that envisions women as feminine, (hetero)sexual objects, and men as masculine, (hetero)sexual subjects.[120]

Certainly, these gender roles create an underlying inequality between the sexes which leads to substantive harassing conduct.[121]

Furthermore, some scholars suggest that sexual harassment is discrimination based on sex because it subordinates women to men.[122] Sexual harassment forces women to be subservient to men because it exploits both their work and sexuality.[123] Heteronormative masculinity encourages the expression of sexuality as power.[124] In other words, male sexual aggression is a societal concern that is caused by a conflation of sex and control.[125] Sexual harassment perpetuates a sexual hierarchy in which men have power on the basis of their ability to define women exclusively in terms of their sex.[126] One scholar suggests a solution to these problems:

---

[118] *Id.* at 1754.

[119] *Id.* at 1755.

[120] Katherine M. Franke, *What's Wrong With Sexual Harassment?*, 49 STAN. L. REV. 691, 693 (1997).

[121] *Id.* at 710.

[122] *See id.* at 725-26 (collecting sources).

[123] *Id.* at 726.

[124] *Id.*

[125] *Id.* at 727.

[126] *Id.* at 728.

> To combat sexual harassment, we must disrupt rather than subscribe to this ambient heterosexism. Whereas the harasser's heterosexism leads him to discriminate by being sexual, the antiharasser's heterosexism leads her to assume that all sexuality [between the sexes] is discriminatory. In both cases, no distinction is made between sexuality and the relation between the sexes. While the harasser is, in one and the same act, sexist and sexual, precisely because he is, we must be able to distinguish sexuality and sexism. And we must always bear in mind that harassment is despicable and illegal, not because it is sexual, but because it is sexist.[127]

Specifically, it is important to eliminate the idea of traditional gender roles and attitudes to restructure ideas about masculine sexuality. Sexuality, or a person's sexual preferences, must remain separate from sexism or sexual prejudice.[128]

Additionally, feminine traits are often devalued to actualize stereotypical conceptions of women.[129] Harassment often focuses on traditionally sexist images of women as fragile caretakers and objects of sexual desire.[130] By insulting these feminine characteristics, the harasser is diminishing their value in the workplace and perpetuating myths about gender roles.[131] However, women who fail to conform to gender norms also experience prejudice in the workplace "for diverging from prescribed notions of appropriate female appearance and demeanor . . . by exhibiting traits commonly associated with men."[132] Indeed, for women and men to be considered wholly equal within our society we must first eliminate these harmful misconceptions about gender and sex.

---

[127] *Id.* at 738.

[128] *Id.* at 746. Sexual discrimination is not an exclusively male to female problem. However, based on research it appears most sexual harassment problems are gendered in this way.

[129] Hillary S. Axam and Deborah Zalesne, *Simulated Sodomy and Other Forms of Heterosexual "Horseplay": Same Sex Sexual Harassment, Workplace Gender Hierarchies, and the Myth of the Gender Monolith Before and After Oncale*, 11 YALE J.L. & FEMINISM 155, 165 (1999).

[130] *Id.* ("Frequently, this harassment centers on stereotypical images of women as physically weak and delicate and as nurturers or sex objects rather than as competent workers. By invoking these traits in an insulting and demeaning manner, the harasser expresses animus toward the presence of devalued, stereotypically feminine characteristics in the workplace.").

[131] *Id.*

[132] *Id.* at 169.

Overall, the ABA is most interested in preserving the integrity of the legal profession. The 2002 addition to Model Rule 1.8 and the 2016 addition to Model Rule 8.4 are examples of the ABA's continued effort to address gaps within the rules. However, both provisions were added to the Model Rules well after the problems that they address were observed. By waiting to change Rule 1.8 and Rule 8.4, the ABA fell behind state jurisdictions in producing innovative ethical considerations. Although the antidiscrimination provision of new Rule 8.4(g) expands the Model Rules in a positive way, the ABA must consider the addition of further details to this rule in order to fully prevent and remedy discrimination.

4

Rule 4.2: Communication Without Representation

Corey Friedman

I. Introduction

Imagine the following scenario: after seven years of collegiate work, you find yourself in a unique situation where you have the knowledge, skills, and ability to represent yourself in a legal matter. However, due to certain restrictions placed on you by the rules of professional responsibility, you are unable to fairly and adequately represent yourself in certain matters. For example, one day you may find yourself in the middle of a divorce. You are knowledgeable in the law, procedures, etc.; however, due to Rule 4.2 of the Model Rules of Professional Conduct (or its state equivalent),[1] you are not allowed to talk to the other party—your own spouse and perhaps even a co-parent—without the presence or involvement of adverse counsel. This poses a problem when attempting to settle the divorce amicably between the two of you, and in making basic arrangements for co-parenting such as scheduling and school matters. Obviously, the presence of opposing counsel can have a soothing effect on the conversation or even act as a point of contention.

Rule 4.2, though actually titled "Communication with Persons Represented by Counsel,"[2] is often called the "no contact" rule. This rule is found substantially in all jurisdictions of the United States.[3] Specifically, the rule states: "In representing a client, a lawyer shall not communicate about the subject of the representation with a person the lawyer knows to be represented by another lawyer in the matter, unless the lawyer has the consent of the other lawyer or is authorized to do so by law or court order."[4] Its root stems from Canon 9 of 1908 ABA Cannons of Profession-

---

[1] AMERICAN BAR ASS'N, MODEL RULES OF PROF'L CONDUCT r. 4.2 (2008).

[2] *Id.*

[3] Geoffrey C. Hazard, Jr. and Dana Remus Irwin, "Toward a Revised 4.2 No-Contact Rule," Faculty Scholarship Series, Paper2323 (2009), http://digitalcommons.law.yale.edu/fss_papers/2323

[4] AMERICAN BAR ASS'N, MODEL RULES OF PROF'L CONDUCT r. 4.2 (2008).

al Ethics, which stated that "a lawyer should not in any way communicate upon the subject of controversy with a party represented by counsel; much less should he undertake to negotiate or compromise the matter with him, but should deal only with his counsel."[5] The rule is geared specifically to the contact between an attorney on one side of a case to the represented client on the other side of said case. The need for the rule stems from the lawyer's increased knowledge of the law, and the lack of knowledge on the part of the client.

One specific topic of Rule 4.2 that I will explore in this chapter is the idea of attorney self-representation and the impact that it has on divorce cases. When an attorney acts as their own counsel, the decision is rendered *pro se*. This signifies in the opinion that the attorney represent-ed themselves in the proceeding. This can create problems in divorce cases where the attorney does not want to, or contact afford to, have outside counsel handle their case.

Additionally, the rule has language about having an exception for communication "authorized by law."[6] Unfortunately, this language does not state what "authorized by law" actually means. The principal explanation of what the "authorized by law" language means is when it comes to cases currently under criminal investigation.[7] The language "authorized by law" originally came from DR 7-104 of the Model Code of Professional Responsibility (1970), known for its ambiguity.[8]

---

5 ABA CANONS OF PROF'L ETHICS No. 9 (1908).

6 AMERICAN BAR ASS'N, MODEL RULES OF PROF'L CONDUCT r. 4.2 (2008).

7 AMERICAN BAR ASS'N, MODEL RULES OF PROF'L CONDUCT r. 4.2 cmt. 4 (2008) pro-vides: "A lawyer may not make a communication prohibited by this Rule through the acts of another. See Rule 8.4(a)." *See also id.*, cmt. 5 ("Communications authorized by law may include communications by a lawyer on behalf of a client who is exercising a constitutional or other legal right to communicate with the government."). It had been previously stated in similar sources that, where authorized by law, government lawyers may advise law enforcement officials about communications with represented parties before the filing of a formal criminal charge or civil complaint against or the arrest of the person in the matter. It is also established that non-lawyer parties to a matter may communicate directly with each other, and attorneys are not prohibited from advising a client concerning a communication that the client is legally entitled to make. Most examples in the Comments and similar sources about "authorized by law" involve such criminal investigative matters.

8 *See, e.g.*, 2 GEOFFREY C. HAZARD, JR. AND W. WILLIAM HODES, THE LAW OF LAWYERING § 38.9 (3d ed. 2001 & Supp. 2008); F. Dennis Saylor IV & J. Douglas Wilson, *Putting a Square Peg in a Round Hole: The Application of Model Rule 4.2 to Federal Prosecutors*, 53 U. PITT. L. REV. 459 (1992); Todd S. Schulman, *Wisdom*

This rule seems to be written in to benefit law enforcement more than any other segment of the legal community. It allows "investigative activities of lawyers representing governmental entities" and "communications by a lawyer on behalf of a client who is exercising a constitutional or other legal right to communicate with the government."[9] This is problematic because while other lawyers must abide by Rule 4.2 in all circumstances, federal lawyers can use law enforcement aiding in the investigation to gather evidence from the opposing side that would be considered to be inappropriate in other circumstances.

Because of this ambiguity, the following analysis will discuss possible limitations to this phrasing and attempt to spell out an exact definition in the context of divorce and similar self-representations.

II. The History of Rule 4.2 in Divorce Cases

The history of Rule 4.2 in reference to divorce cases is well represented. Traditionally, judges in divorce courts prefer for spouses to attempt to work out their differences together. This proves to be tricky when one spouse is a lawyer representing themselves, because in those cases they may not be able to freely communicate with their spouse without legal counsel present. Rule 4.2 only applies when a lawyer is "representing a client."[10] It does not specify whether it applies to a lawyer who is acting *pro se*, such as a lawyer communicating directly with his landlord in a dispute over a lease or a lawyer communicating directly with a spouse in a divorce proceeding. In these and similar situations, lawyers have a legitimate interest in being treated as fairly as any other party to the matter. Opposing parties, meanwhile, have legitimate interests in the rule's intended protections.

The following will dive into this topic and propose a reform to Rule 4.2. This reform would allow attorneys who self-represent to freely speak with their spouse, through the use of a so called "bad faith" clause. The bad faith clause would act as a fail-safe to ensure that the attorney does not take advantage of the opposing spouse. An example of a case where a

---

Without Power: The Department of Justice's Attempt to Exempt Federal Prosecutors from State No-Contact Rules, 71 N.Y.U. L. REV. 1067, 1074-78 (1996).

[9] AMERICAN BAR ASS'N, MODEL RULES OF PROF'L CONDUCT r. 4.2 cmt. 5 (2008).

[10] *Id.*, r. 4.2.

lawyer took advantage of this and acted with bad faith is *Vickery v. Commission for Lawyer Discipline.*[11] The basic facts of this case are that Glenn Vickery was a very prominent attorney in his area.[12] This prominence allowed him and his wife to buy numerous properties and assets. Vickery then became embroiled in a malpractice case. Fearing that his malpractice insurance would not cover a judgment levied against him, he hatched an idea to stage a divorce with his wife to protect half of his assets. After explaining the idea to his wife, she objected due to their happy marriage. Trusting the word of her husband, Mrs. Vickery agreed to proceed with the divorce. She did not have a hand in any of the matters of the divorce, even choosing to skip the court date for it. After the divorce was finalized, Mrs. Vickery discovered that Mr. Vickery had married her best friend and that he had begun the process of evicting her and her daughter from their main residence. She also discovered that instead of splitting assets 50/50 like he said he would, he instead took a significantly disproportionate percentage of the assets.

This case highlights the need for the "bad faith" requirement. Mr. Vickery knowingly took advantage of his advanced knowledge of the law to defraud his wife. Ultimately the courts in the bar discipline case threw the book at him and suspended him from practicing law for three years, as well as sanctioning him with a substantial fine. If the courts had not chosen to pursue the matter, or if Mrs. Vickery had not filed suit on the substantive matter, Mr. Vickery would have gotten away with a significant amount of fraud.[13]

Rule 4.2 does, however, allow lawyers to contact opposing sides when there is a dispute where opposing side would not ordinarily retain a lawyer.[14] One example would be where a lawyer/consumer whose suit is ruined by a dry cleaner may contact the dry cleaner directly, instead of going through the dry cleaner's legal counsel.[15] This exemption was put in place to ensure that a lawyer was not unfairly treated. To take away the

---

[11] Vickery v. Commission for Lawyer Discipline, 5 S.W.3d 251 (Tex. App. 1999).

[12] *Id.* at 252.

[13] *Id.*

[14] D.C. Bar Association, "Ethics Opinion 258," Apr. 12 2017, http://dcbar.org/bar-resources/legal-ethics/opinions/opinion258.cfm

[15] *Id.*

ability for lawyers to mitigate some sort of damage would result in taking away their ability to protect their assets.

A. History of Rule 4.2

Rule 4.2 has historically been used to protect a client from unlawful intrusion by the opposing counsel.[16] Because of attorneys' advanced knowledge of the law, it can be easy for them to use this knowledge to take advantage of the opposing side. In order for an attorney to communicate with opposing client, they are required to have either the presence of opposing counsel or approval from opposing counsel. Gaining approval from opposing counsel is rare, as there really is no upside to not being present, other than to perhaps to save time.

Rule 4.2 began as Cannon 9 in the 1908 ABA Canons of Professional Ethics.[17] The original Canon stated that "a lawyer should not in any way communicate upon the subject of controversy with a party represented by counsel; much less should he undertake to negotiate or compromise the matter with him, but should deal only with his counsel."[18] Canon 9 was essentially a rule of evidence, and its "no-contact" concept was much more limited than the eventual Rule 4.2. Case law under the Canon generally focused on whether "concessions or admissions obtained directly from a represented person should be denied legal effect."[19]

After the introduction of the ABA's Model Code of Professional Responsibility in 1970, the rule was expanded into today's no-contact ideal.[20] The rule, DR 7-104(A)(1), would eventually become today's Rule 4.2 of the Model Rules of Professional Conduct. It originally stated that a lawyer should not "communicate . . . on the subject of the representation

---

[16] *Id.*

[17] ABA Canons of Professional Ethics No. 9 (1908).

[18] *Id.*

[19] *See, e.g.,* Coughlan v. United States, 391 F.2d 371, 376-78 (9th Cir. 1968) (Hamley, J., dissenting); Reinke v. United States, 405 F.2d 228, 230 (9th Cir. 1968); United States v. Smith, 379 F.2d 628, 633 (7th Cir. 1967); United States v. Ferguson, 243 F. Supp. 237, 238 (D.D.C. 1965); Juskowitz v. Hahn, 56 Misc. 2d 647, 648 (N.Y. Sup. Ct. 1968); State v. Nicholson, 463 P.2d 633, 636-37 (Wash. 1969). *But cf.* ABA Comm. on Ethics and Prof'l Responsibility, Formal Op. 108 (1934) (referring to Canon 9's broad prohibition).

[20] *See* Hazard and Irwin, *supra* note 3, at 799; MODEL CODE OF PROF'L RESPONSIBILITY DR 7-104(A)(1) (1969).

with a party he knows to be represented by a lawyer in that matter unless he has the prior consent of the lawyer representing such other party or is authorized by law to do so."[21] Courts viewed this rule as a way to protect the layperson who lacked the knowledge and training to protect themselves. Eventually, the rule became a strict interpretation to include all communications, written, oral, or direct, to an opposing client.[22] This interpretation has been maintained through the years to become the traditional Rule 4.2 that we abide by now, as implemented by virtually all state bars. The current instance of Rule 4.2 includes that same strict interpretation and is extremely rigid in its protections.

One way that Rule 4.2 contributes to the proper functioning of the legal system is by protecting a person who has chosen to retain representation.[23] The writers of the rule were concerned that a lawyer with advanced knowledge of the law may coax out information and overstep their bounds.[24] They designed the rule to make sure that the layperson is protected against predatory practices by the lawyer. This protection is afforded even if the represented person initiates or consents to the communication.[25] If such a contact is made without opposing counsel's consent, the lawyer must immediately terminate communication with that person once they discover that the party is under representation.[26]

The interesting part of this rule, and one focus of the proposed change to the rule, is that the rule does not prohibit communication with a represented individual if the communication concerns something outside of the case at hand.[27] An example would be if there is a legal dispute between an attorney and one of his workers. Once the worker retains legal counsel, the attorney can no longer speak with him about the issue. If he decides to communicate about a separate issue, perhaps a golf game, he is under no penalty under 4.2. Rule 4.2 also does not prohibit a client from seeking the legal opinion of an attorney who is outside of the case at

---

21 MODEL RULES OF PROF'L CONDUCT R. 4.2.

22 Hazard and Irwin, *supra* note 3, at 800.

23 *See* D.C. Bar Association, "Ethics Opinion 258," Apr. 12 2017, http://dcbar.org/bar-resources/legal-ethics/opinions/opinion258.cfm

24 *Id.*

25 *Id.*

26 *Id.*

27 *Id.*

hand.[28] It does however prohibit a non-involved party from making comments on behalf of a relationship that would be considered to be in violation of Rule 4.2.[29] This does not, however, preclude opposing parties in a case from freely communicating about the case.[30]

In the situation in which a lawyer is uncertain whether a communication with a represented person is permissible, they may seek a court order to determine what would be considered acceptable.[31] A lawyer may also seek a court order in exceptional circumstances to authorize a communication that would otherwise be prohibited by this rule. For example, it may be necessary to have a communication with an opposing side to avoid foreseeable harm.[32] This could be something along the lines of a corporation's allowing an affected party to retain their in-house counsel, not understanding that the counsel may have the corporation's best interests at heart, not those of the defendants.

Additionally, the drafters designed the rule to cover any communications with any person who is represented by counsel in the matter that the communication concerns.[33] This means that any communications between opposing counsel and client relating to the issue at hand is prohibited. This becomes tricky during divorce cases where the attorney represents themselves. Rule 4.2 is quite silent on the matter but the Third Restatement allows for an exception for a "lawyer who is a party to the matter and who represents no other client in the matter."[34]

III. Addition of Specific Language

Rule 4.2 is considered overly broad and ambiguous.[35] The purpose of the rule is to protect against overreaching and deception of non-clients.[36]

---

28 *Id.*

29 *Id.*

30 *Id.*

31 *Id.*

32 *Id.*

33 *Id.*

34 RESTATEMENT (THIRD) OF THE LAW GOVERNING LAWYERS § 99(1)(b) (2000); *id.* § 99 cmt. E.

35 *See* Hazard and Irwin, *supra* note 3.

The rule was left intentionally ambiguous to allow for more protection of the layperson against lawyer misconduct. It also has a hidden purpose of protecting the attorney-client privilege because it prevents a lawyer from obtaining privileged information from opposing clients.[37] The California Supreme Court, in describing Rule 4.2, has stated that "[t]he rule was designed to permit an attorney to function adequately in his proper role and to prevent the opposing attorney from impeding his performance in such role."[38]

Rule 4.2's protections also extend beyond the scope of the attorney-client privilege. Applied strictly, Rule 4.2 effectively protects represented individuals from all informal interviews and investigations.[39] This privilege is extremely important and prevents a layperson from accidentally revealing information that could be detrimental to their case.[40] Because of this, this chapter proposes that there be specific language added to the rule to make it more specific in regards to *pro se* representation, with a focus more on the "attorney-client privilege" aspect, as well as setting a definition to the "authorized by law" section of the rule.

First, one idea that I propose comes from Geoffery Hazard and Dana Remus Irwin's 2009 paper entitled "Towards a Revised 4.2 No-Contact Rule." In this paper, the authors proposes that the rule be changed to focus more on the "attorney-client privilege, not just the benefit of the attorney or the client."[41] This proposal is one that I believe is an excellent one. It would allow for the preservation of the attorney-client privilege, while at the same time allowing for the opposing attorney to communicate with the opposing client, in good faith. This also allows for proper functioning of the legal system because Comment 1 of Rule 4.2 states that it protects the "proper functioning of the legal system by protecting a person who has chosen to be represented by a lawyer."[42] This gives a

---

[36] RESTATEMENT (THIRD) OF THE LAW GOVERNING LAWYERS § 99(1)(b) (2000); *id.* § 99 cmt. E.

[37] Hazard and Irwin, *supra* note 3.

[38] *As quoted in* ABA Comm. on Prof'l Ethics and Grievances, Formal Op. 108 (1934); *see also* United States v. Lopez, 765 F. Supp. 1433, 1451-52 (N.D. Cal. 1991).

[39] *See* ABA Comm. on Prof'l Ethics and Grievances, Formal Op. 108 (1934).

[40] Hazard and Irwin, *supra* note 3, at 800.

[41] *Id.* at 804.

[42] AMERICAN BAR ASS'N, MODEL RULES OF PROF'L CONDUCT r. 4.2 cmt 1 (2008).

protection to the consumer who chooses to solicit the services of an attorney, thus continuing the profitability of the profession.

Second, the wording in the rule in regards to certain communications being allowed that are "authorized by law" is ambiguous—and there seems to be the ability to use that ambiguity to claim an unfair advantage in proceedings. However, the rule was arguably limited with the ruling of the "McDade Amendment," which stated that although "an attorney for the government shall be subject to the state rules and laws, it still does not preclude federal prosecutors from such a rule."[43] The purpose of this amendment was to apply state-level no-contact rules to federal prosecutors. Commentators have noted significant differences between the activities of state and federal prosecutors, however, rendering this approach problematic.[44] The problem that this produces is that most federal investigations are made by law enforcement officers that are not subject to Rule 4.2. This is not a problem shared by lawyers in self-representation cases nor ones of divorce.

Because of the ambiguity, the change I am proposing is to specifically limit the range in which a federal attorney may contact an opposing client. The way to promote this solution is to include language that an attorney may not use law enforcement to contact an opposing client on their behalf. That way, all communications with law enforcement may be used, so long as they are given voluntarily by an opposing client.

The reform to the rule to include specific language is a preferable alternative to keeping the rule at status quo. The addition of language to define that of *pro se* representation, proper contact with non-legal parties, as well as setting a definition to the "authorized by law" section of the rule, will help to limit the ability of a well-trained lawyer to take advantage of an untrained layperson.

---

43 *See* 28 U.S.C. § 530B (2006). The Amendment provides: "An attorney for the Government shall be subject to State laws and rules, and local Federal court rules, governing attorneys in each State where such attorney engages in that attorney's duties, to the same extent and in the same manner as other attorneys in that State." The effect of the Amendment is to apply state no-contact rules to federal prosecutors just as they apply to state prosecutors (and to all other lawyers).

44 Fred C. Zacharias and Bruce A. Green, *The Uniqueness of Federal Prosecutors*, 88 GEO. L.J. 207, 216 (2000); Note, *Federal Prosecutors, State Ethics Regulations, and the McDade Amendment*, 113 HARV. L. REV. 2080, 2090 (2000).

IV. Reform Proposal in Divorce Cases

Another reform that I am proposing is to expand on the allowed communication, specifically in relation to divorce cases. The rule should be worded to allow for spouses to communicate in reference to a settlement, without legal representation, with consent from the overseeing judge. Due to the lack of material written on the subject, it would seem reasonable to assume that under the mantle of good faith, open dialogue between spouses would be a good thing. In addition, a clause for "bad faith" dealings should be enacted, which would only be triggered if it is found that the lawyer-spouse used their advanced legal knowledge to dupe or defraud the opposing spouse.

Because most divorce courts attempt to have the parties work out their issues amicably, it would seem like having parties not able to communicate would be counterproductive to this goal. The proposed change would allow both sides to communicate freely and attempt to work out a settlement amicably. In a traditional non-lawyer, *pro se* case, the courts recognize that the ability to represent oneself is a fundamental right.[45] The parties are not restricted by any rules of professional conduct. In this case, the enforcement of those professional rules would appear to create a hindrance on lawyers who choose to self-represent. It would follow common sense that lawyers should not be hindered by a law due only to the fact that they have advanced training.

V. "Bad Faith"

One of the proposed reforms for Rule 4.2 is the inclusion of a "bad faith" clause requirement in regards to attorney self-representation in divorce cases. The need for this stems from the idea that a lawyer, with their advanced knowledge of the law, has the ability to use this knowledge to deceive a spouse into doing something they would not agree to do if they knew what they were agreeing to. "Bad faith" as outlined would be to intentionally deceive the spouse.

An example of why this is necessary would be that of a divorce case where open dialogue is needed to maintain a civil split. Imagine that in a divorce, for anything you needed to communicate about, you would have

---

45 Maxwell v. Maxwell, 375 S.C. 182, 650 S.E.2d 680 (Ct. App. 2007).

to go through opposing counsel. Not only is this a recipe for a very expensive divorce, it would also give the proceeding a very businesslike tone. Instead of a civil conversation, the lawyer would be there to make sure that the couple did not say anything counsel did not like. This creates a lack of cooperation and can drag out the proceeding, potentially making it very ugly. Reforming the rule would provide an ability for the lawyer and their spouse to communicate more freely, and the change would hopefully allow the processing to be civil and more productive for both sides of the issue.

The need for a "bad faith" requirement stems from an ability of legally trained attorneys to leverage their legal knowledge to take advantage of their lesser-trained spouse. This is highlighted in the Texas case of *Vickery*, in which Glenn Vickery used his knowledge as an attorney—and apparently his powers of persuasion—to take advantage of his wife during their divorce.[46] His wife trusted him to do what was right for the both of them and he used this trust to defraud her out of her share of the assets. He was found to be in violation of Rule 4.2, but only in the sense that he communicated with her in regards to the pending "divorce." Had he not communicated with her about divorce proceedings, he would have been able to get away with taking advantage of her ignorance of the law. Because of this, the "bad faith" requirement would be an invaluable addition to the protection of non-lawyer opposing parties.

This proposed rule protects the layperson from predatory practices that can stem from a difference in education level or experience. Lawyers are generally in a better position, due to their education, training, and understanding of the law, "to overwhelm a lay party and exploit his lack of legal knowledge in the course of communicating directly with the lay party."[47] And allowing a lawyer to have free rein over an opposing side creates the risk, among other abuses, of the lawyer's using their knowledge to receive privileged information that the client did not intend to disclose.

For example, imagine a lawyer who is representing themselves in a case about workers' compensation against the lawyer-employer. In a regular instance of this new Rule 4.2, the lawyer could speak with the

---

[46] *Vickery*, 5 S.W.3d at 253.

[47] D.C. Bar Association, "Ethics Opinion 258," Apr. 12 2017, http://dcbar.org/bar-resources/legal-ethics/opinions/opinion258.cfm

harmed party. The lawyer, being versed in workers' compensation laws, could potentially give bad advice or make offers to the client for significantly less than they are legally entitled to. This may cause irreparable harm to the opposing client. The "bad faith" requirement would likely be triggered in this instance, especially if the judge in the case sees that the lawyer knowingly gave bad advice and leveraged their knowledge of the law to give intentionally bad advice.

This requirement would also allow courts to monitor the practices of lawyers and weed out the ones who use their advanced knowledge to take advantage of a disadvantaged individual. Allowing a lawyer to have free rein over their conduct would be detrimental to the interests of the opposing party.

VI. Effect on the Legal Profession

With this new proposal, there will be an obvious effect on the legal community, specifically the community of divorce attorneys that represent clients who are acting in opposition to lawyers who represent themselves. Divorce attorneys make a substantial portion of their money from representing clients in negotiations and mediation sessions. The reform would put a dent in their personal profits, but in the realm of public good, it is a rational idea to implement this strategy.

The public good of this proposal would be that there would be a more rational understanding of Rule 4.2. With more of an understanding about "authorized contact," lawyers will be able to understand what their client will go through in the process of their case. With the new reform on divorce, lawyers representing themselves will be able to make contact with their spouse to finalize their divorce in more of a civil manner. The "bad faith" proposal would ensure that lawyers who use their advanced knowledge of the law to take advantage of others are thwarted or reprimanded.

VII. Conclusion

To conclude, Rule 4.2 is an important rule to protect non-lawyer clients from being overwhelmed by attorneys. Attorneys have advanced training in the law and have the capacity to take advantage of the ignorance of a layperson. Because of this, lawyers are not allowed to communicate directly with an opposing client without the presence of their representation. This proves quite tricky in divorce cases, where an opposing client may be your spouse.

The proposed changes to Rule 4.2 would allow lawyers who represent themselves in divorce cases to speak with an opposing client. This allows for a more open dialogue which will in most cases lead to a more amicable decision. The rule would also be changed to preserve the attorney-client privilege to allow for the proper functioning of the legal system in most other instances.

Additionally, the language of Rule 4.2 in regards to allowing contact that is "authorized by law" should be amended to not allow federal attorneys to take advantage of a lack of a no-contact clause for them. While the rule has since been amended, the lawyer is still allowed to make inappropriate contact through the law enforcement officers that make the investigations and discoveries. This is an issue because, in regard to knowledge of the actual laws, the law enforcement officers are on about the same level as the opposing side. Rule 4.2 should be amended to disallow the federal attorney from using the law enforcement officer to discover things that would be considered privileged in other Rule 4.2 instances.

There still, of course, needs to be a protection against attorney mis-conduct. This is why there should also be implementation of the proposed "bad faith" threshold. In this way, a practitioner could be reprimanded if they act in a way that knowingly takes advantage of the other side. This would, in theory, prevent an attorney from taking advantage of a spouse-client in the same way that played out in *Vickery*.

Finally, the effect on the legal profession as a whole would be minimal. While a large portion of divorce lawyer billable hours come from mediation, depositions, etc., the effect on the legal profession overall would be positive. There would remain plenty of billable hours for the lawyers themselves in representation, motions, divorce planning, and other topics.

PART TWO

International and Comparative Perspectives

5

Law Placement of International Students in U.S. Law Firms

Qinyu Fan

The United States has seen an obvious increase in the enrollment of international full-time J.D. students, from 1.70% in 2009 to 2.45% in 2013.[1] Although most foreign law students are enrolled in LL.M. programs, the increase in the enrollment of full-time J.D. programs shows an advanced ambition of foreign lawyers in the United States.

The increasing presence of foreign lawyers in U.S. law firms began in the mid-1990s.[2] Because most legal practices in the U.S. require foreign lawyers to have a U.S. law degree and pass the bar exam, many foreign law students decided to take law programs in U.S. law schools to conduct cross-border legal practices or even to pursue their careers in the U.S. There are two major reasons attracting foreign lawyers to come to the United States: one of them is the global expansion in law practice activities, and the other is the value of U.S. legal education and the high quality of legal services. Therefore, even though foreign law students are still a very small group, their future law placement and career prospects are important in this new trend. This chapter will consider their career development as well as their roles in the U.S. legal service market, and further explore how this market should react to the increasing presence of foreign law students.

I. Varied Expectations of Foreign Law Students

Legal services in a country is a career highly related to its national systems, which creates an inevitable barrier for many foreign law students

---

[1] ABA Approved Law School FT Total Enrollment by Gender and Ethnicity Data Page, http://www.americanbar.org/content/dam/aba/administrative/legal_education_and _admissions_to_the_bar/statistics/2009_2013_ft_total_jd_enrollment_gender_eth nicity.xlsx (last visited Mar. 17, 2017) (Excel spreadsheet compiled by ABA).

[2] Carole Silver, *The Case of the Foreign Lawyer: Internationalizing the U.S. Legal Profession*, 25 FORDHAM INT. L.J. 1039, 1042 (2002).

to practice law in the United States. On the one hand, while the U.S. common law system is developed by case law or precedent,[3] there are a lot of countries, such as Germany, France, Japan, China and Spain, practicing civil law. In this way, because of its leading position in international business, the United States attracts a large group of foreign law students from different legal systems with its law school programs; however, on the other hand, most states in the U.S. do not recognize the eligibility of a foreign law degree.[4] Therefore, legal education in the United States is required for those foreign law students who want to practice law in the United States or to conduct cross-border legal activities.

Foreign students who come to law school in the U.S. have highly varied features based on their culture background, different legal knowledge, and language skills, as compared to U.S. law graduates. Consequently, their interest and goals in the U.S. legal service market are diversified.

Some foreign law students come to the U.S. with the incentive to be able to better practice law in their home countries. Most of them will choose LL.M. programs in the United States, rather than J.D. programs. For example, those foreign law students who want to practice law in international settings will choose to further pursue a U.S. law degree. Firstly, advanced legal services in the U.S. teach them a commonly used legal language in the global legal service market. Secondly, many "elite firms that serve international businesses" in foreign countries, for example, Germany, "have affiliated or merged with Anglo-American law firms."[5] Having a U.S. law degree or even the working experiences in the U.S. makes those foreign law students highly distinct in working in those law firms in their home countries.[6] In this case, not only is a U.S. LL.M. degree helpful, a J.D. degree is even more valuable. However, except for the strict job gatekeeper for potential future lawyers, the law school admission is also a difficult process. Twenty years have passed since the mid-1990s, at which point increased numbers of foreign students started

---

[3] Wikipedia, *Common Law*, https://en.wikipedia.org/wiki/Common_law (last visited Apr. 27, 2017).

[4] *International Students Becoming a Lawyer in the United States*, Lawyeredu.org, http://www.lawyeredu.org/international-law-students.html (last visited Apr. 27, 2017).

[5] Silver, *supra* note 2, at 1040.

[6] *Id.*

to enroll in U.S. LL.M. programs and enter into the U.S. legal job market; since that time, foreign students have had access to much more information about U.S. law schools. Therefore, after the first generation of foreign LL.M. students, there are increasing numbers of foreign students who choose to apply for J.D. programs.

As an indication of intelligence and analytical ability, U.S. law degrees help those foreign law students improve their human capitals, and as a result make them more competitive in the law society in their home countries. For some other foreign law students, the threshold of entering the legal service market is even higher than it is in the United States. "Students from Taiwan, Japan, and Korea commonly fall into this category because of the extremely low bar passage rate in these countries."[7] Since passing the bar exam is usually a basic requirement for practicing law in most countries, those foreign law students choose to get a U.S. certificate in practicing law to enter the legal service market.

Thus, the purposes of foreign law students chasing a law degree in the United States vary highly among members of this small group. Additionally, after they come into contact with the real world, their views may change quickly as they gradually know more and more about the legal society, which will probably change their expectations of their own law career.

II. Why and Why Not Hire Foreign Law Students?

Among international law students, many are attracted by the opportunities and challenges in the U.S. legal society. Considering working in U.S. law firms as a valuable experience, even "those [LL.M. students] who begin the year with no intention of staying beyond their nine months of course work often decide to consider temporary assignments in the United States."[8]

Those foreign students who work in the United States as a lawyer will fall into two categories. One of them is foreign law students who are hired in a specific section in the law firm, often related to their international background or based on their multiple language skills. The other category

---

[7] *Id.* at 1050.

[8] *Id.*

is foreign law students who works in the same way their native fellow law students do.

A. Hiring Foreign Students Specialized in International Legal Practices

For the first group of foreign law students, the market value is still uncertain even though nowadays everything is becoming more and more globalized.[9] The general opinion given by the U.S. legal society, according to James Maxeiner, is that "credentials in the international area are secondary to being a solid, talented practitioner."[10] Thus, as a matter of fact, the current need of hiring foreign law students to deal with international legal issues is still very limited. Maxeiner's article offers several reasons for this current situation of not always hiring foreign law students despite their advantages in their international background.

First is the dominant role of the U.S. legal system and English.[11] Consistent with the United States' dominant role in daily international business, in most cases, the barriers in different legal systems and foreign language will not be a big problem. It is true that when it comes to a legal issue in an international background, English will probably be the dominant language. A U.S. lawyer who goes abroad to deal with foreign lawyers in other countries does not have to speak their language because in most cases, qualified translators are easily found. The differences in legal systems might be a harder issue. But many of the international business cases will go to an international arbitration tribunal, which is governed by international law and available to both foreign and domestic lawyers who are specialized in international law. In some other business cases—for example, international arbitrations—the concept of transnational arbitral procedure attempts to impart some independent legal status to an award that is rendered in compliance with an agreed regime of international arbitration rules, which corresponds to the effective reality of how the parties intend the arbitral process to work.[12] In this

---

9 James. R. Maxeiner, *International Legal Careers: Path and Directions*, 25 SYRACUSE J. OF INT'L L. & COM. 21, 23 (1998).

10 *Id.* at 28.

11 *Id.* at 29.

12 W. Laurence Craig, *Some Trends and Developments in the Laws and Practice of International Commercial Arbitration*, 50 TEX. INT'L L.J 699, 701 (2016).

way, if an international case goes to a court in any country, the parties have the right to come to an agreement on the court's location, which means that the U.S. party effectively has the right to pick a favorable location of the relevant court. The rest of international cases will go to an international court of justice and are governed by laws of that international organization, assuming there are no treaties that resolve the jurisdictional issue. Where there is some necessity that the jurisdiction should be managed under the governance of international law, the U.S. Constitution directly invokes international law or concepts of international law in clauses ranging from the treaty and war powers to commerce and citizenship.[13] Thus, the legal barriers among different legal systems are mostly resolved inherently by the international laws and treaties that supply the law of the substantive matter. By learning international law, a U.S. law student who focuses on international law will be able to resolve most of the international legal issues with lawyers from other countries, according to the prominent view on whether to hire international law students.

However, considering the current small population of foreign J.D. students, hiring a competent foreign law student will potentially save human and material resources. On the one hand, legal interpretation requires the translator to have at least some degree of understanding of the legal language. The cost of hiring translators for legal services will be higher than using regular translators and a foreign law student will be the best choice, because law firms don't have to hire a translator. On the other hand, legal practice under an international background does not equate to the use of international law. A lot of transaction cases are settled, which is generally resolved in a more complicated context related to cultures and ideology in the other country. In this way, in the long run, hiring international law students can reduce the cost and at the same time achieve a better result.

Second, the contribution of an international background is not obvious.[14] In the most extreme example, in the international litigation process, each party usually provides arguments from the perspective of their legal system, or the shared international legal system, which

---

[13] Sarah H. Cleveland, *Our International Constitution*, 31 YALE J. INT'L. L. 1, 8 (2006).

[14] Maxeiner, *supra* note 9, at 29.

requires little knowledge of the other country.[15] However, legal services are not limited to litigation practices. Appropriate communications with diverse clients are also crucial. After all, the value of the legal society is reflected in the quality of its services. Although the core competences and reputation of a law firm are the main factors in attracting its clients, providing better services for diverse clients does increase the value of the law firm in the long run. In addition, the ability to attract big international clients will largely expand the client sources of a law firm and makes it more competitive in the competitive legal market. Conceptually, it is understood that if the international background of a foreign law graduate is well used, it certainly will increase the value of the law firm.

The third factor is the professional self-interest in existing lawyers.[16] Some might mention that, since globalization is still a new trend, though developing quickly, young and new associates might be more interested in this area than senior attorneys. Thus, there is a chance that more experienced lawyers will forbid further communications between foreign law students and their respective clients from the same country.[17] However, this can be proven to be generally wrong because, according to a survey among foreign LL.M. students, international law students from "small and economically insignificant" countries are less likely to be successful in working for U.S. firms,[18] in which case there is less potential self-interest.

But there may be another more reasonable explanation for this delayed phenomenon. The well-established legal education and the popularly shared values existing in the employment of law school graduates act slowly in this trend, with the small group of competent international students. In this case, firm leadership plays an important role in international expansion. When firm leadership has had international exposure, this increases the extent of internationalization of the firm.[19] After the employment of international students, large law firms with international legal practices, such as Cleary Gottlieb, White & Case,

---

[15] *Id.* at 30.

[16] *Id.*

[17] *Id.* at 31.

[18] Silver, *supra* note 2, at 1064.

[19] Winfried Ruigrok and Hardy Wagner, *Internationalization and Performance: An Organizational Learning Perspective*, 43 McMT. INT'L REV. 63, 68 (2003).

Sullivan & Cromwell, Davis Polk, and Baker & McKenzie, continue to hire more and better foreign law students who have received a U.S. law degree. Most of them are among the first generation of law firms who react to this globalizing trend and now, among their employers, there are more and more competent foreign law students who graduate from top law schools in the United States. Among those firms, Sullivan & Cromwell is a global leader in M&A and represents clients worldwide on their largest and most important domestic and cross-border transactions.[20] Over the last ten years, the firm has advised on approximately USD $4.20 trillion in announced transactions worldwide, including many of the largest and most important transactions in the United States, Europe, Latin America, and Asia. And White & Case is listed as the fifth in Chambers Global Top 30 law firms.[21]

In conclusion, international legal services are still not the core business in most of the U.S. law firms. Therefore, whether to prefer a foreign law student because of their international background in their international legal service section depends on their goals. If a law firm targets itself to enter the global legal service market, the sooner it will start a plan to hire competent law students, the better result they will achieve. At the same time, the group of international law students is still small but is developing quickly, which will lead to a more and more competitive market even among international law students. Therefore, I am optimistic about hiring competent law students according to their needs and plans in global legal practices.

B. Hiring Foreign Law Students as Substitutes for U.S. Law Students

This trend usually applies to international J.D. law students because U.S. attorneys have some standardized skills they obtained at law school, for instance, legal writing, analyzing, and research. Most of the U.S. students who want to practice law in the United States are trained in three-year J.D. programs before they are prepared to be a lawyer. When

---

[20] *Global Practice Guide for Corporate M&A 2017*, ChambersandPartners.com, http://practiceguides.chambersandpartners.com/practice-guides/corporate-ma-2017 (last visited Apr. 26, 2017).

[21] *Chambers Global Top 30*, ChambersandPartners.com, http://www.chambersandpartners.com/global-comparisontable (last visited Apr. 26, 2017).

hiring foreign law students as substitutes for U.S. law students, law firms are looking for similar competences in them. "The source of this competence may be their U.S. law school experience, their English language ability, as well as other experiences that prepare them for practice."[22] In this case, even in a relatively small number, more and more foreign law students are enrolled in top law schools in the United States. While studying abroad costs them a lot of money and they usually need to conquer more barriers in the application process than their American peers, few of them will go to less competitive law schools, which will give them less successful career in the future. Thus, even though this is a small group, foreign law students in the long run may have more potential opportunities if they gradually overcome barriers in American culture and society.

To foreign LL.M. students, there is an even larger gap between them and the market demand even though they have earned a foreign law degree. A hiring partner stated: "U.S. law school is hardly sufficient preparation for working at a U.S. law firm—there's a substantial disconnect between law school and law firm practice, but the disconnect would be larger if the lawyer was foreign-educated. That would make the work of a law firm seem even more foreign than it already does to new associates. . . . [When foreign lawyers] are hired, they tend to be a pace or two behind U.S.-educated lawyers. A U.S. LL.M. degree is not a good substitute for a J.D. degree."[23] However, some LL.M. students still successfully found jobs working as substitutes for their American peers. Those cases are usually highly dependent on their personal qualities, experiences at law school, and the law firms. Generally, successful foreign lawyers working in a law firm as other American lawyers should be considered as individual cases. Foreign legal background and law degrees usually will not help too much in this case.

Because of the dominant position the United States has in the global market and the legal field, the diverse backgrounds that foreign law students have do not help them very much in law firms. But considering the increasing number of upcoming foreign J.D. students, more and more foreign law students are joining in the fierce competition in the legal service market. And due to the smaller job market and more impediments

---

[22] Silver, *supra* note 2, at 1065.

[23] *Id.* at 1075 (quoting view of hiring partner in firm of more than 500 attorneys).

they will face while pursuing their legal career in the United States compared to their American rivals, the competition among foreign law students in the U.S. job market as well as the enrollment in top U.S. law schools will be increasingly intense. The potential market for foreign law students and their competitiveness will have a mutual effect on each other as a result of the growing population of this group of law students.

Law, today, still remains "stubbornly local," even in spite of "the importance of economic globalization."[24] And this localized character of legal systems "reduces the harmonizing impact that globalization has generated in other sectors of the economy."[25] Whether this situation needs to be changed is an even broader topic. The legal service market is not only highly local and domestic, but also regionally stubborn. Even within the U.S., many law firms will prefer law graduates from local law schools. For example, students who graduated from St. John's are more likely to find a job in New York than law students from a law school outside with a slightly higher ranking, in part because of the influence of the school's alumni.

However, if you think about the recent history of Constitutional Law, as regards its use of the law of nations, there might be some enlighten-ment on this issue. International and foreign sources in constitutional analysis once invoked Justice Clarence Thomas for the proposition that "this Court ... should not impose foreign moods, fads, or fashions on Americans."[26] But gradually the Justices have explained their more recent willingness to look abroad for multiple reasons: adjudications on similar questions, globalization, and the universality of basic human rights.[27]

Similarly, from an employer's perspective, whether to hire a foreign law students should mostly depend on the value he or she could bring to the firm. And their value should be seen in a more comprehensive way, i.e., their overall abilities to bring profits to the law firm based on a global vision, but not only in a traditional way. No matter if the current view on this issue is healthy or not, employers will not change their perspectives until foreign law students start to bring large profits to the firm. Thus, for

---

[24] Carole Silver, *Local Matters: Internationalizing Strategies for U.S. Law Firms.* 14 IND. J. OF GLOBAL LEGAL STUD. 67, 68 (2007).

[25] *Id.* at 67.

[26] Cleveland, *supra* note 13, at 3.

[27] *Id.* at 5.

foreign law students, the chances that they get hired by law firms will go up if they are competent in legal kills and are able to provide law firms with valuable human resources.

III. Potential Jobs for Foreign Law Students

Other than the motives law firms have in hiring foreign law graduates, there are some other resources which can help foreign law students to find the right position in this legal service market.

First, both J.D. and LL.M. students can join the campus recruiting activities generally held in all top law schools. They are fully exposed to as many job opportunities as their American classmates.

Secondly, law firms with international legal market demands will join foreign lawyer job fairs. Such job fairs are often held in more diverse regions where foreign lawyers tend to work, for example, New York, Chicago, Washington, D.C., and California. In those regions where foreign law students have opened up their practicing area, law firms are more likely to consider hiring foreign lawyers and to be familiar with the conditions. However, although there are a lot of organizations and associations across the United States, the purpose of most of them are not recruiting foreign law students, but do provide them with potential opportunities to get contacts with law firms.[28] Some of the organizations are nationwide, including related departments in the American Bar Association, American Society of International Law, International Law Students Association, International Bar Association, International Municipal Lawyers, and Inter-American Bar Association.[29] Some of them are more local, such as the Foreign Lawyers Association of New York. Those associations or organizations will hold conferences in regions mentioned above, and advertise those conferences online and among law firms with international business demands. In this way, those associations do provide some extent of help to foreign law students, but not directly. They mainly play two roles in helping foreign law students to obtain a job. One of them is bridging the information gap between law

---

[28] Silver, *supra* note 2, at 1054.

[29] *See generally Career Opportunities in International Law*, Glenn.OSU.edu, http://glenn.osu.edu/career/guides-resources/career-guides/Career%20Opportunities%20in%20International%20Law.pdf (last visited June 21, 2017). Another potential resource group is the American Foreign Law Association, http://afla-law.org/.

firms and foreign law students who have fewer connections in the United States, compared to American law students. The other one is to provide practical advice from successful lawyers with an international background or directly from hiring partners in law firms. However, those connections are vulnerable and hard to build. Even in law firms conducting international legal services, compared to their demands for lawyers in domestic legal practices, the demand for foreign lawyers is much smaller. Thus, law firms will not value connections they build in foreign lawyer job fairs too much in their recruiting activities and this approach plays a non-obvious role in helping foreign law students to land a job in the U.S. legal service market.

Third, foreign law students from countries the U.S. has important business relations with are more likely to find solid personal connections to help them to land a job in a U.S. law firm.[30] Those personal connections, such as connections with a foreign client in a U.S. law firm, play a role in keeping foreign clients or even bringing future revenues to the law firm. Although this seems to be a practical approach for job research of foreign law students, it does not play such an important role to law firms, either. According to a foreign law student from China, whose uncle is an existing considerable client of a big U.S. law firm, hiring partners have not taken serious consideration in hiring him after his graduation from the J.D. program at U.C. Davis.[31] It is hard to find an existing connection solid enough between foreign law students and a law firm to increase their job opportunities. However, another Chinese law student found connections leading to a successful job, landing in a large law firm during her law school study in the United States. Part of the reason she successfully found a job in the U.S. legal service market is due to her excellent achievement in the J.D. program, having transferred to Yale Law School and participated in the Law Journal there.[32] Not to mention her distinctive ambition and hard work during law school.

Building connections in the U.S. legal society is extremely challenging because of the culture gaps and short stay during law school. But it is not

---

[30] Philipp Lassahn, *How to improve your chances of landing a job in the US after your LL.M.,* LLMGuide.com, https://llm-guide.com/articles/post-llm-career-focus-the-us-job-market (last visited Apr. 27, 2017).

[31] Personal anecdote known to this chapter's author.

[32] Personal anecdote known to author.

impossible and still depends a lot on foreign law students' personal attributes including their academic achievement and social ability. In addition, a personal connection plays a more important role in providing a job opportunity when it is related to ethnicity. There are many examples among minority lawyers in the United States. Yery Marrero, who made "partner at Marrero Borzorgi and received her J.D. from Loyola University New Orleans College of Law in 1988," was "welcomed and supported by the small and growing Hispanic legal community, which became critical to my growth as a lawyer."[33] There, "one of the only Cuban judges introduced [her] to a Cuban supervisor at the public defenders' office, where [she] started [her] first job" and finally made a success.[34] This case further shows the potential job opportunities in the future that a foreign lawyer could create for upcoming international law students after some of them achieve their success in the legal field.

Last but not least, online information provides foreign law students with an effective and efficient pool of potential opportunities in the U.S. legal service market. On popular job research websites, such as the Best Law Firm list in *U.S. News & World Report*, jobs can be narrowed to the international section and a list of law firms with existing or potential international legal practices can be easily found. Foreign law students could start their job research from there. Also, job hunting websites targeting at international law students will be helpful. For example, on *www.indeed.com*, there are around 600 jobs available for foreign law students directly posted by employers. This channel offers foreign law students classified information from across the United States and makes it easier for their job hunting. It also provides a more direct channel for both foreign law students and law firms that have a demand for international law lawyers. However, this is not the way law firms prefer in employing law graduates and therefore is not the most efficient way to locate a foreign law student in the U.S. legal service market. Furthermore, many of these websites are not authorized by a solid national legal association and have a limited way to advertise themselves. On the one hand, the reliability of the information on these websites will be easily

---

33 Aviva Cuyler, *Diversity in the Practice of Law: How Far Have We Come?*, AmericanBar.org, http://www.americanbar.org/publications/gp_solo/2012/september _october/diversity_practice_law_how_far_have_we_come.html (last visited Apr. 27, 2017).

34 *Id.*

questioned. On the other hand, it is hard to build up its reputation and attract users. Thus, information on many of these websites is not reliable nor thorough enough for legal job research.

Those channels of job research for foreign law students who want to work in the United States are not exclusive to each other. For example, foreign law students could also build connections on websites such as *LinkedIn*, particularly the Top Law Schools forum. Such sites play a crucial role in finding a job in the United States especially for foreign law students because of their popularity and reputation, and their extensive information resources.

There is another special job opportunity for foreign law students. With the trend of global legal services, a lot of U.S. firms start their business overseas. Those U.S.-based international firms prefer to locate foreign law students in branches they have in their respective home countries. With their U.S. legal education background and advantages in dealing with domestic business in their home countries, foreign law students are their best choices to deal with cross-border legal issues overseas. Many international LL.M. students successfully landed their job in this way. Conversely, foreign law firms that have branches in the United States offer international law students good opportunities to work in the U.S. legal service market targeting their international clients based on their home countries. In both cases, international students with a U.S. education background will know the local market better compared to their colleagues and, in this job setting, those positions are more exclusive to international students than jobs in the domestic legal practices in the United States.

In conclusion, potentially international law students have fewer job opportunities in the U.S. legal service market than their American peers, because of their short stay and limited experiences in the United States. It will be much harder for them to obtain an appropriate job in this market through common channels shared with U.S. law students at their law school. However, their combined experiences in legal field and culture background will offer them more channels in job researching. Compared to common channels, such as law school recruiting, positions offered in accessary channels are much less prevalent but are more focused on international students. Those channels still need to be improved to adapt to this steadily increasing group of international law students, if the law society wants to better locate jobs for international law students.

IV. Potential Ends of Foreign Lawyers

Since the substantial legal practices international students in the U.S. started less than 20 years ago, it is still too early to give a solid conclusive answer to the potential development and ends of foreign lawyers' careers. In 1999, the most recent year for which information is available, 2,287 individuals who attended law school outside the United States sat for the New York bar examination; 43% of these students passed the exam.[35] Therefore, among the first generation in this small group, some of them may have worked in a U.S. law firm for more than ten years.

However, until now there have not been many successful cases of foreign international students making extremely successful careers such as becoming a senior partner in large U.S. law firms. One of the reasons is probably because most of them are LL.M. students, who, even though they had passed the bar exams, were less competent in the traditional view as being a promising lawyer in their future career. One other reason is probably because it was hard to open this cross-border legal service market and create the demand for international lawyers in a U.S. law firm. As mentioned above, the U.S. legal system has been a matured and developed legal system for a long time, and it is hard to accept a brand-new group of competitors with different backgrounds in all aspects unless they have made eye-catching contributions to U.S. law firms. This is understandable because during the past 20 years, changes are happening every day, and a lot of the changes would affect the U.S. legal society. For example, the rise of information technologies has brought historically important change to the society, including the legal service market. And even the better position of women and the minority group of lawyers in this market is not fully resolved. The law placement of international lawyers in U.S. firms is only one of the changes and is still a new one. And being an international J.D. student myself, I am still frequently asked about the reason why I came here to study law. It shows that even at a law school where the society accepts changes faster, this is still a new trend, and the contributions or changes they brought to the U.S. legal society have not been obvious yet. However, will they bring substantial change to the U.S. legal society? The answer is still uncertain and we could only guess.

---

35 Silver, *supra* note 2, at 1058.

This partly explains why there are not many successful international lawyers in the U.S. legal society yet. However, I have an optimistic attitude towards the future contributions they will make. This is because the major problems facing foreign lawyers are related to the knowledge of this new society. These problems can be conquered after years of studying and working in the United States, if those international students realize those problems and actively adapt themselves to this new environment. Even if they are currently behind compared to their American peers, in the long run, their experiences and ability to adapt to a new environment will help them in catching up. From my personal experience, coming from a civil law country, on the one hand, the U.S. legal service market is attractive because, for example, it provides me better opportunities to better practice law, and studying in a J.D. program at a U.S. law school is a valuable experience to learn about the legal system in another country. There are thousands of reasons that have driven me here to study U.S. laws. However, on the other hand, the barriers in language skills, daily social life, and cultural differences are hard to overcome, which has consumed a lot of energy during my highly-pressured law school life here.

This trend of increasing foreign law students in the United States, I would say, will continue, and this group of people, who have overcome a lot more barriers, has the potential to do better in the long term. And if law firms are more open to this trend, they will bring valuable cultural resources to law firms to achieve more benefits. From the examples of new international lawyers, only those who are extremely hard-working and smart made their way to succeed in becoming an associate in large law firms. And they are working even harder in U.S. law firms because they appreciate the position they have won, especially those international students who are working as substitutes for U.S. attorneys.

Speaking of those international lawyers who are working as substitutes for U.S. attorneys, apart from this subjective factor, an objective factor that may bring success in their future career is their additional skills and knowledge, which was a subordinate factor during their job-hunting process. Being employed in large firms means that they already are competent enough in the core skills from the law firm's perspective, and with this global trend, their multiple language skills and other subordinate advantages in the job hunting process will bring them more chances in the future. Therefore, they will probably gradually bring changes to the law firms in the long run.

Speaking of those international lawyers who work on legal business related to their international background, the future career is much more uncertain. Some of them are temporarily hired, because some international students have the goal to study law, get working experiences in the United States, and return to their home countries as a more competitive lawyer there. Their job expectation is also increased. For J.D. students, they are more likely to bring U.S. clients in their home countries to their law firms there and make considerable contributions. In this way, they will benefit a lot from their U.S. law study and working experiences and are more likely to become a partner in their law firms. For LL.M. students, they are more likely to focus on a special area, mostly related to international business, where big profits generate. However, due to the large population of foreign law students in U.S. LL.M. programs, fierce competition is facing them even in their home countries, especially in the countries the United States has substantial international business with. For example, among excellent lawyers in China, a U.S. LL.M. degree is not highly distinctive anymore.

Nevertheless, this advantage will still guarantee that those international students will be a good lawyer there. Some other international lawyers who work on legal business related to their international background will choose to stay in U.S. law firms. Their career in the future will be even more uncertain because of the entry of increasing numbers of international law students. They may be more likely to be replaced by other, more competent, international lawyers. However, their working experience and the cost of replacing them will also be an obvious advantage in their future career. After all, the training in U.S. law firms is considerably important as is their legal education background. Therefore, their future careers will depend significantly on how much they learn from working experiences. The market demands in this legal section is not large now and the development space is probably small, according to the previous analysis. Even if there is any space, it can be easily filled up by upcoming international law graduates who will be more competent in the increasingly fierce competition. And they will have the least opportunities to become a core partner in a U.S. law firm, because the legal section in which they specialized is too narrow.

Speaking of international lawyers who are working in a branch of U.S.-based international law firms in their home countries, they are more likely to have a bright future as well. Working in their home countries with a U.S. legal education background makes them competitive there. And their working experiences there are hard to be replaced because they are more likely to be partly in charge of the cross-border international business in the legal field. This will make them more and more distinctive even compared to the upcoming international law graduates from the United States.

In conclusion, the future career of an international lawyer remains highly dependent on how much they will learn from their daily business. However, as compared to the future career of American lawyers in U.S. firms, there are more factors affecting the international lawyer's future and it varies a lot depending on the path they choose. Those factors include their U.S. legal education background, the job they choose, and the upcoming competition among international lawyers within the United States.

V. Opportunities and Obstacles

The biggest opportunity for international law students in the United States lies in the areas where the globalization trend in the legal field will benefit the most to U.S. law firms. The benefits brought by the increasing number of clients from foreign countries are secondary and not so obvious. Benefits of investments from big clients overseas will directly affect the U.S. economy, which will make the relations with foreign clients increasingly important. However, as mentioned above, the United States is often the dominant party in international transactions and, because of the inherent strength in the U.S. legal service market, legal services from U.S. law firms are important to foreign clients. Those big foreign clients usually have high demands on legal services, and most of them will choose large U.S. international law firms. Based on the twin facts that even big foreign clients cannot afford to lose their U.S. market, and legal services provided by large U.S.-based law firms are competitive with their experienced lawyer teams and the inherent strength in the U.S. legal services, those large international U.S.-based law firms often do not worry so much about creating job opportunities for international law students to maintain a healthy relationship with their international clients. Chart 1 shows the dominant position U.S. law firms have in the global legal service market.

Chart 1 ▪ Ratio of Local Firms to All Top Firms[36]

Practice	China	France	Germany		Italy	Japan		UK		US
Corporate M&A Top 1st-3rd Tier Practices[1]	3/17	7/19	3/9		5/6	0/18		6/6[a]	5/8[b]	16/16
Corporate M&A Top 4th-5th Tier Practices[1]	0/11[c]	2/10	2/11		13/16	N/A		N/A	4/12	11/11
Capital Markets Top 1st-3rd Tier Practices[1]	0/15	2/13	1/6[d]	1/8[e]	3/9	0/12[f]	6/9[g]	6/12[d]	7/7[e]	10/10
Capital Markets Top 4th-5th Tier Practices[1]	2/8	2/4	0/4	0/1	N/A	N/A	N/A	0/2[d]	1/7[e h]	5/5

1. These ratios reflect total corporate/M&A deals or international corporate/M&A deals, depending on the specifics of the country rankings.

a. Larger Deals/Larger Resources

b. Larger Deals/Medium Resources   *(Notes continue)*

36 D. Daniel Sokol, *Globalization of Law Firms: A Survey of the Literature and a Research Agenda for Further Study*, 14 IND. J. OF GLOBAL LEGAL STUD. 5, 10 (2007). Data are originally from *2006 Chambers Global Guide.*

    c. Two firms are non-US/UK

    d. Capital Markets Debt

    e. Capital Markets Equity

    f. Foreign Capital Markets

    g. Capital Markets

    h. Five of six foreign firms are U.S.-based, the other is French-based

From the chart, we can tell that most of law firms overseas are under attack by their U.S.-based competitors, particularly for high-end deal work,[37] and when a foreign client comes to "shop" in the U.S. legal service market, most of them will choose a U.S.-based law firm. However, theoretically, the foreign capital market is itself alluring enough to make U.S. firms start their international expansions, and as a result, they should be more actively hiring competent international lawyers from their clients' home countries because that helps them to attract big foreign clients. The main reason for the gap between the theory and the reality is that the internationalization of a firm comes with costs and benefits, because international firms must reconfigure their internal systems to respond to the process of internationalization.[38] And in keeping these foreign offices open, law firm management at these firms believes that at some point these offices will make a profit,[39] but in practice, many law firms lose money in their foreign operations.

Thus, the potential revenues that the increase in foreign clients will bring to the U.S. law firms can create opportunities for international law students but, currently, not in a substantial way. Here I am going to further analyze the reasons behind this gap. According to Daniel Sokol's article, noted above, there are mainly three types of global expansion models for law firms. They are greenfield expansion, which occurs through new entry and organic growth, and allows for revenue capture by a single firm; alliance among law firms; and expansion via merger or acquisition. Greenfield expansion is chosen currently by most law firms because of the lowest transactional costs. However, it will cost more to create the local offices overseas in the long run, reducing the potential

---

[37] Sokol, *supra* note 36, at 11.

[38] *Id.* at 12.

[39] David L. Deephouse, *To Be Different, or To Be the Same? It's a Question (and Theory) of Strategic Balance*, 20 STRATEGIC MGMT. J. 147, 147-48 (1999).

profitability of law offices in foreign countries. Forming an alliance with foreign law firms will not directly bring profits to the firm. A firm can also expand through the merger or acquisition of a preexisting firm or a group of lawyers from a preexisting firm.[40] International expansions through M&A will reduce the cost to build new offices, conduct research on local legal service market, etc. The largest barrier a law firm expanding its market overseas will encounter is the cultural differences between its offices in foreign countries and its offices in the United States. Thus, among those three types of international expansion, the M&A international expansion is the most profitable, in my opinion, because it will bring more profits to U.S. law firms with lower costs.

Expansions in the global legal service market will bring more revenues to U.S. law firms than attracting foreign clients to come to the United States, in general, because this works more directly on increasing their revenues. Additionally, the potential capital market for law firm international expansions is much larger than the market of deal work brought by foreign clients who would like to expand their business in the United States.

In this way, both opening their business in foreign countries (i.e., greenfield expansion), and conducting M&A activities with foreign law firms, will create more potential opportunities for foreign law students in the United States. In fact, at present, greenfield international expansions have created most job opportunities for foreign law students in the U.S. According to the job research published in *U.S. News & World Report*, the listed major firms hiring international law students are mostly U.S. law firms that have branches overseas, and their posted job opportunities are accordingly facing international law students from those countries. Therefore, international expansion in legal business market overseas has been proven to be effective in creating job opportunities for international law students. Additionally, there is another profitable way of international expansion for law firms that has not been fully explored.

The international expansion of law firms, which began in earnest in the 1980s, has transformed large law firms.[41] Among those expansions, the M&A form of expansion started a little bit later. In a recent example, within five years two little-known regional law firms merged, added three

---

[40] Sokol, *supra* note 36, at 13.

[41] *Id.* at 5.

smaller firms by merger, doubled in size through another merger in October 2004, and in January 2005 completed an international merger with an English firm to create the world's third-largest law firm, with more than 2,700 lawyers at forty-nine offices in eighteen countries.[42] The international merger, by Piper Rudnick LLP (with main offices in Chicago and Baltimore) and London-based DLA, created a firm that was behind only Clifford Chance and Baker & McKenzie in number of attorneys. With projected annual revenues of $1.5 billion, it is second only to Clifford Chance.[43] This example has led to aggressive international expansions through M&As among law firms.[44]

This rising trend of M&A activities among international law firms will certainly bring more opportunities for international law students in the United States. Different from opening new businesses in foreign countries, through M&A activities, U.S.-based law firms are exposed to a larger potential market and will save the cost of entering a new market overseas, by using the entities and personnel there.[45] Therefore, expansion through M&A will bring more benefits in this globalization trend of the legal service market. Furthermore, after the M&A activities, there will be more business between the targeted foreign legal market and the legal service market in the United States, which will further create connections between the U.S. legal system and those in the foreign countries. Therefore, compared to the job opportunities brought by opening business in foreign countries, the increasing M&A activities will give U.S.-based law firms a real motive to be actively involved in this globalization trend in the legal field and will therefore create more future opportunities for international students in the United States.

However, speaking of the most troublesome obstacles encountered by international law students who intend to find a job in the U.S. legal service market, their citizenships—and the complicated and costly process

---

[42] Bruce E. Aronson, *Elite Law Firm Mergers and Reputational Competition: Is Bigger Really Better? An International Comparison*, 40 VAND. J. OF TRANSNAT'L L. 763, 765 (2007).

[43] Martha Neil, *A Mondo Merger: Piper Rudnick Teams with London's DLA to Get Really Big, Really Fast*, A.B.A. J. E-REPORT, Dec. 10, 2004, *cited in* Aronson, *supra* note 42, at 765 n.1.

[44] Aronson, *supra* note 42, at 765.

[45] John Grimley, *What opportunity do law firm mergers in Asia create for foreign law firms?*, AsiaLawPortal.com, https://asialawportal.com/2015/11/16/what-opportunity-do-law-firm-mergers-in-asia-create-for-foreign-law-firms/ (last visited Apr. 27, 2017).

before being able to work in U.S. firms—are major difficulties for law firms to hire them. This is another important reason that U.S. law firms are more reluctant to consider international law candidates compared to U.S. law graduates.

As one career training guide notes, "All U.S. employers are subject to the restrictions of U.S. immigration law. This means that employers may only hire individuals who are eligible to be employed. To be considered 'eligible' for employment, LL.M (also J.D.) students must be (1) citizens of the United States; (2) aliens who have been lawfully admitted to permanent residence ('green card holders'); or (3) individuals expressly authorized for employment by U.S. Citizenship and Immigration Services, Department of Homeland Security."[46] Considering the current policies, U.S. employers are faced with even more strict conditions by sponsoring foreign law students work visas.

Thus, the cost of hiring new international law candidates is not limited to the human and material resourcing in recruiting and training law graduates, but also in the process of dealing with their citizenships. Moreover, according to the policy on H-1-B visas, which are required for permanent work of international lawyers, even if U.S. law firms are willing to spend resources on recruiting and training them, and sponsor them for their visa, they still have a limited chance to be able to work for the firm. This is because, after the application for an H-1-B visa, only 20,000 out of all the graduate international applicants holding U.S. advanced degrees could obtain the visa. On U.S. law firms' behalf, why invest so much to hire someone who needs to run a national lottery before he or she could really work for them? This is happening in interviews with law firms as well. Among the questions in the interview, law firms need to find out if an international student satisfies the prerequisite of being legally permitted to work in the United States before they make any further decisions. And that will increase the threshold of hiring an international law student. Furthermore, the immigration policies change every now and then, and are thus hard to predict, which make it even more risky for U.S. law firms to hire international lawyers. In this way, to be hired in a U.S. law firm, international law students need to be not only as competent as their American peers, but substantially more competent.

---

46 *Career Planning Guide for the Foreign Trained Attorneys*, Law.WUSTL.edu, http://law.wustl.edu/career_services/docs/careerplanningguideforeigntrainedattorne ys.pdf (last visited July 21, 2017).

VI. Conclusion

Nowadays, the opportunity for U.S. legal education has been increasingly opened to international law students. However, this group of law students is faced with a tense situation in the U.S. legal service market—partly because of their insufficient experiences in the United States, partly because of the market demands and the policies. In addition, the difficulties and unknowns of immigration remain a substantial roadblock to law firm hiring.

Nevertheless, although the current demand for international law students is not so obvious, in the long run, hiring international law students can substantially increase law firms' revenues. To achieve this goal, both international law students in the United States and those ambitious U.S. law firms must work together. International law students should actively work harder on conquering their weaknesses and prove more value to law firms, while ambitious U.S. law firms are working on their plans to positively react to this international change in the global legal society.

6

Development of the Legal Profession in China

Shu Chen

I. Introduction

A. Current Situation

"Legal profession" is a relatively new term in China, especially in the People's Republic of China. When the Chinese Communist Party started to govern the country, it ignored the ideal of legal justice for a long time. As a result, the legal profession did not have healthy development. After Chair Deng Xiaoping started to govern the country, he focused on opening the country and making it more international. Now, during these years, with the quick economic development, people in China have started to use lawyers more and the leaders of the country have emphasized the development of the legal system and its legal profession.

As a result, law schools in China gradually have become popular, and more families choose to support their children to go to law schools during their undergraduate education. And there is a large population of students who continue to pursue their masters and doctorate degrees in law since they want to become more competitive in the legal job market. With higher standards of legal education and the support of the country's policy to develop China's legal system, there is an expectation by many lawyers and legal scholars in China that the legal environment in the country will become better and better in the near future.

B. An Overview of the History

The word "lawyer" only appears in modern China. In the ancient Chinese judicial system, the "legal pettifogger" played an important role as lawyer. Legal pettifogger, equivalent to the Chinese word "song shi," can be traced back to the Western Zhou Dynasty. They were treated more as impudent shysters. This system lasted nearly 3,000 years in China until the Qing Dynasty.[1] At that time, the word "lawyer" first appeared in the Civil Procedure Code of the Grand Qing Dynasty, which was drafted by Wu Tingfang and Shen Jiaben in 1910. Later, in 1912, the Beiyang government of the Republic of China enacted the Provisional Act of Lawyer. This Act regulated lawyer qualifications, lawyer certification, lawyer registration, lawyer duties, bar association, and punishment.[2]

During the period from 1912 to 1949, the legal profession developed gradually. Legal thought was highly affected by Japan and Germany during this period. In 1949, the People's Republic of China was established, then its legal profession was deeply affected by the decade-long Cultural Revolution from 1966 to 1976. In 1980, the Provisional Act of Lawyers of People's Republic of China was enacted; it is the first law of modern China which regulates lawyers and the legal profession.

In July 1986, the first national lawyer conference was held in Beijing. An Article of national bar association was passed during the conference and a national bar association was officially established.[3] In 1996, the general offices of the National People's Congress passed the Law of the People's Republic of China on Lawyers. It has amended in 2012. In 2004, Code of Conduct for Lawyers was passed in the 9th executive council meeting of the national bar association. This law regulates the modern Chinese lawyer's profession and activities in most of the parts. On December 20, 2015, General Office of the Communist Party and General Office of the State Council distributed their Opinion about improving the national legal profession qualification system, which aimed to make Chinese lawyers professionalized.

C. The Path to Becoming a Lawyer in China

In China, the key path to becoming a lawyer, a judge, or a prosecutor is to take the national judicial examination. The examination is held annually, and candidates have to meet some requirements: the candidate

---

[1] Study of traditional Chinese "song shi" culture, Jiangzhou Dang.

[2] This Act specified that only males of the Republic of China held the qualification to be a lawyer. A candidate could be admitted to be a lawyer by successfully passing the bar exam, or a candidate could be exempted from taking the exam if he had satisfied some further requirement in this Act.

[3] Retrospect and prospect—the development history of Chinese lawyer in one hundred years, Zhang Zhiming.

must hold Chinese nationality, uphold the Constitution of the People's Republic of China, and have the right to vote and be voted on. The candidate should graduate with a bachelor of law degree from a university or college. If the candidate graduates from a university or college without the bachelor of law degree, he or she can still attend the judicial exam as long as he or she has knowledge related to law. The candidate should have good character.[4] There is no strict regulation about whether or not candidates have knowledge related to law. So if you have no formal knowledge of law, but you feel that you can learn it by yourself, you can attend the judicial exam. This exam started in 2002 and there were 36,000 candidates that year. The full score of the exam is 600 and the passing score was 240 at that time. But two years later, the passing score became, and was kept at, 360 every year. The passing rate of the exam is very low. See the chart below for passing rates from 2002 to 2015.[5]

Year	2004	2005	2006	2007	2008	2009	2010	2011	2012	2013	2014	2015
Pass Score	360	360	360	360	360	360	360	360	360	360	360	360
Pass Rate (%)	11.2	14.4	15.0	22.4	27.0	35.0	14.3	16.0	12.0	11.0	10.0	10.0

Between the time the candidate passes the exam and he or she becomes a lawyer, there are some other things to do. The candidate needs to do an internship in a law firm for one year. During this internship period, the candidate has to submit application materials to the judicial bureau for which he or she does the internship. Also, there will be an interview after the candidate passes the review of the application materials. After the candidate successfully passes all of these, the last step is to submit materials about being a lawyer to the judicial bureau. Finally, the candidate is officially a lawyer when the judicial bureau gives notice to him or her to receive the lawyer license.

---

4 http://www.moj.gov.cn/sfkss/content/2008-08/14/content_923585.htm?node=301, Department of National Judicial Examination.

5 http://learning.sohu.com/20161122/n473796865.shtml. Autonomous Regions have a lower pass score for those exam candidates whose place of registration is an Autonomous Region at the time of their applying for the exam.

D. The Path to Becoming a Judge in China

For pursuing a career of judge in China, the candidate needs to pass the national judicial examination. Besides this, the candidate also has to sit for the civil service examination-judge position held by the public security authorities. Test-takers have two hours to answer 135 multiple-choice questions on topics covering language, mathematics, logic, politics, law, and culture. That is followed by three hours of essay questions.[6] After passing the exam, there is an interview, which is to test the test-taker's cognition about the civil servant's job function. Following the interview are a physical examination and political examination. In the political examination, the employment department of the court for which the test-taker applied will check the criminal and political background of the test-taker.[7] A prerequisite to being a judge is having legal work experience for two years, and this time requirement is three years for the higher people's court and supreme people's court. Candidates with a master of law or doctor of judicial science degree only require one-year work experience. The work experience stated above includes the time the candidate spends during his or her internship when he or she was at school.

With the implementation of the 2016 system reform of the specified number of judicial personnel, courts all around China started to cut down on the number of judges to guarantee the balancing quota of judges and cases. As a result, the new person who starts to work at a court probably has to wait a longer time to be a judge since as the number of the judge is fixed: no addition of a judge is necessary when the number is satisfied.[8]

II. Code of Conduct of Lawyer

Code of Conduct of Lawyer regulates the general ethics rules applicable to lawyers in China.[9] Code of Conduct of Lawyer was first reviewed

---

6 *Could you pass China's grueling, 5 hour civil service exam?*, http://www.cnn.com/2016/11/28/asia/china-civil-service-exam/

7 http://www.chinagwy.org/html/xwsz/zyxw/201606/21_160455.html

8 *Judicial Reform in China 2016*, http://www.chinagwy.org/html/xwsz/zyxw/201606/21_160455.html

9 Code of Conduct of Lawyer is not the only law that regulates lawyers' practice in China. Administrative Measures for the Practice of Law by Lawyers is another law that regulates lawyers' conduct during practice. It was first issued in 2008 by the Ministry

and provisionally passed on the 9th Executive Council meeting of the national bar association in January 2007. In 2009 the Code was revised by the second session of the seventh council, on December 27, 2009. This Code has nine chapters (and 108 articles in all), including general provisions, lawyers' basic practice norms, lawyers' norms for promoting business, regulations of the relationship between lawyer and client or parties, standards for lawyers involved in litigation or arbitration, norms for lawyers' relationships with other lawyers, norms for lawyers' relationships with their law firm, norms for lawyers' relationships with lawyers' associations, and supplementary provisions.[10]

The national All China Lawyer Association Executive Council has the right to interpret and explain this Code and will explain it for applications of this ethics code. The Executive Council also has the right to revise and amend it. However, Code of Conduct of Lawyer does not regulate punishment against lawyers who violate the Code; rather, the punishment method for violations is regulated by Law of People's Republic of China on Lawyers, which was drafted and revised by the standing committee of the People's Congress in October, 2007.

A. Lawyer Advertising

Chapter III Section 1 Article 15 of Code of Conduct of Lawyer provides that in promoting their practice, lawyers and law firms shall abide by the principles of equality and good faith, shall abide by lawyers' professional ethics and discipline, and shall abide by recognized industry standards and fair competition. The Code provides that both lawyers and law firms may use advertisements to lawfully promote the firm or lawyers and their practice areas and strengths. Lawyers publishing advertisements shall comply with national laws, regulations, rules, and the Code's further specifications. Lawyers publishing advertisements shall be identifiable, and the social public shall be sufficiently able to recognize that it is a lawyer advertisement. Lawyer advertisements may be published in the lawyer's own name or may also published in the name of a law firm. Lawyers ads published in the name of an individual lawyer shall clearly

---

of Justice of the People's Republic of China. Then it was revised in 2016. This law not only regulates the lawyer's conduct, it also regulates the qualifications to be a lawyer.

[10] *See* http://www.chinalawtranslate.com/lawyers-practice-code-of-conduct-draft-revisions/?lang=en

note the name of the lawyer's practice organization, and shall clearly indicate the lawyer's license number.

Lawyers and law firms, in any of the following situations, must not release a lawyer's advertisement: (1) did not pass the annual assessment; (2) during the period of punishment where practice has been stopped or suspended for rectification; (3) it has been less than a year since receiving a criticism notice or public censure. The content of lawyers' advertisements shall be limited to the lawyer's name, image, age, gender, education, degrees, specializations, the date on which they became permitted to practice law, the name of the law firm where they practice, the period of their time as a lawyer in the firm, their fee standards, contact information, the scope of legal services they may provide, and practice achievements. The content of a law firm's advertisements shall be limited to: the name of the law firm, its location, telephone number, fax number, mailing address, e-mail and website; the lawyers' association it belongs to; the lawyers practicing with the firm; and a brief introduction to the legal services they can provide to the public and practice accomplishments. Lawyers and law firms must not advertise in a style contrary to mission of lawyers or harmful to lawyers' image, and in creating advertisements they must not adopt the artful exaggeration techniques used in ordinary commercial advertisements. Content violating the lawyers' association's provisions related to advertisement management must not appear in lawyer advertisements.[11]

In the real world, sometimes it is hard to tell whether the law firms are at fault with their law firm's advertisement on websites that are operated by a third party. For example, as of early March, 2017, there is a law firm advertisement case in Beijing related to violation of the advertisement law and Code of Conduct of Lawyer. A law firm in Beijing put on several law-related websites ads with slogans such as "professional lawyers, top brand in housing demolition and relocation lawyers," "dispute resolution success rate No. 1 all around the country." The person in charge in the law firm stated that they did not realize the existence of these slogans written in this way because they contracted with the related website to make and operate these ads. Several days later, the websites with those illegal slogans disappeared. The law firm released claims that all the firm's ads on those related websites were attacked by unidentified

---

[11] *Id.*

hackers and after they noticed the problem they immediately required the third party to inspect and fix the problem. And the person in charge stated that the websites resumed normal operation again. But the law firm did not positively state anything about the illegal ads on these websites; they avoided admitting to the ads. Further investigation revealed that in this law firm, there was a lawyer who was ranked in the top 100 lawyers in China, but then staff in the Supreme Court's newspaper office investigated the ranking contest and wanted to know how the top 100 lawyers are chosen. The staff found out that the contest was a scam. The contest organizers are non-lawyers, even having no person in the general area of law.[12] In China, for the lawyer's illegal ads, both the judicial bureau and industry and commerce bureau can give punishment; however, like the situation in this case, it seemed there was no evidence to prove whether it was a hacker attack or the law firm intentionally put on the ads. So it will make it difficult to decide to punish the law firm. The lack of law to deal with the situation leaves risk to harm potential clients' rights.

Local rules and laws in different areas and provinces may be a little different from Code of Conduct of Lawyer's regulations. For example, in Beijing, it is regulated in the Measures for the Administration of Beijing Law Firm Law Practice Advertisement that the law firm is the only party that can be an advertiser; lawyers personally cannot advertise. The contents of the advertisement are limited to: name of the law firm, office address, phone number, fax number, post code, e-mail address, website, and the legal services that it can provide. The contents of the advertisement cannot include: false information; contents that express or imply that the law firm has a special relationship with government agencies, community organizations, intermediaries and their members; contents of client lists, cases, and achievements; contents related to honors or self-complimentary; contents that depreciate other law firms or lawyers; contents that make a commitment to or guarantee of case results; contents offering no charge or lesser charge; contents on education, degree, title, and social duties; and any other contents that relate to unfair competition.[13] Tianjin also bans individual lawyers from advertising their

---

[12] *A law firm in Beijing is suspected of releasing illegal ads*, http://mt.sohu.com/20170314/n483314731.shtml (previously available as of March 21, 2017).

[13] Measures for the Administration of Beijing Law Firm Law Practice Advertisement, https://www.zhihu.com/question/22021583

practice, like the situation in Beijing, largely limiting the free competition between lawyers. Although there are cities like Guangzhou and Shanghai that do allow both individual lawyers and law firms to advertise, the limitations in other areas push lawyers who cannot make legal advertisement to use some illegal ways to expand their practice, such as giving business cards in court or near the court areas, which will not leave a good impression of lawyers to the public.

The ban of individual lawyers in publishing advertisements makes it hard for people who need legal services to locate a suitable lawyer. The bureau's officer that released this ban argues that the advertisement market in China is not mature enough to let lawyers individually to make advertisements and that there are many illegal advertisements that have damaged lawyers' image in public. So the bureau still thinks that it is necessary to ban individual lawyers from making advertisements. Also in China, unlike in the United States, people do not need lawyer as much as Americans do, and when a real need comes, most people prefer to get a lawyer whom they know or get a recommendation from a relative or friend. From this perspective, at least, we can see the reasonable point of the ban on individual advertisements.

By comparison to U.S. laws, Chinese laws regulating lawyer adverting are very general. Code of Conduct of Lawyer does not distinguish prospective clients and non-prospective clients and says nothing about the behavior of solicitation of clients. And the form of advertisement is not regulated, leaving open the question of whether or not television and internet advertising is allowed. Also, laws are lacking regarding lawyer referral. As stated in the above paragraph, instead of banning individual lawyers from advertising, a more specific law works better. Take recent news in the U.S., for example: the chairman of the House Judiciary Committee is asking the ABA to amend its model ethics rules to require a disclaimer in attorney ads that seek plaintiffs who have been injured by pharmaceuticals.[14] The disclaimer should advise patients not to discontinue medication before consulting their physician, according to U.S. Rep. Bob Goodlatte.[15] According to Rep. Goodlatte's letter written to the ABA,

---

[14] Debra Cassens Weiss, *US lawmaker wants ethics rules to require warning in legal ads seeking drug plaintiffs* (March 14, 2017, 12:29 PM), http://www.abajournal.com/news/article/us_lawmaker_wants_ethics_rules_to_require_warning_in_legal_ads_seeking_drug (last visited June 26, 2017).

[15] *Id.*

the onslaught of attorney ads has the potential to frighten patients and place fear between them and their doctor. By emphasizing side-effects while ignoring the benefits or the fact that the medication is FDA-approved, these ads jeopardize patient care. For many patients, stopping prescribed medication is far more dangerous, and they need to be looking out for them.[16] The letter asked the ABA to respond by March 21, 2017, and at the time of this writing the ABA has received the letter, is looking at the issue, and intends to respond before the due date. No matter what may be the ABA's response, amendments such as this should be encouraged to avoid lawyers' misleading or even frightening contents in ads.

In practice, lawyers in China have found many more methods to advertise. Many lawyers take advantage of online advertising; they create legal websites and legal blogs to enhance their practice publicity, and the charge of creating legal websites is not very high—around less than 500 Yuan a year (USD $72). Legal blogging is also very efficient and is free of charge; some lawyers also believe that the online bulletin board system is an effective advertising tool. Many lawyers open a QQ or WeChat account,[17] using an identifiable name so that people can know they are lawyers, and lawyers in this way enlarge the number of potential clients.[18]

B. Confidentiality of Information

Law of the People's Republic of China on Lawyers Article 38 provides that a lawyer shall keep confidential state secrets and a client's commercial secrets learned during practice. Code of Conduct of Lawyer Chapter II Article 8 further provides that lawyers shall keep confidential the state and trade secrets learned during practice, and they shall not reveal their client's privacy. Lawyers shall keep confidential the client's and other persons' circumstances and information learned during the representation, which they do not wish to be revealed. However, there is an

---

[16] *Quoted at* https://judiciary.house.gov/wp-content/uploads/2017/03/Letter-to-ABA.pdf?utm_source=House+Judiciary+Committee+Press+Releases&utm_campaign=0d66e4a097-
EMAIL_CAMPAIGN_2017_03_07&utm_medium=email&utm_term=0_df41eba8fd-0d66e4a097-101865929

[17] QQ and WeChat are the most-used instant messaging software in China.

[18] *How lawyers advertise in China—a Guangzhou lawyer's thoughts*, http://wenku .baidu.com/link?url=tHESAacF1jgno1ISWDohpS4Z7CB6L-OhWskraPWmz5gZ PQTNd3TyCjNggMi0XAVOlNipXHxk6oteZ_VI8kb-U3ef3xY1nMAv55yB0-vd12_

exception for facts and information regarding a client or other person's preparation for, or current engagement in, crimes that endanger state or public security, or seriously endanger the personal safety or others or their property.

Although the new Law of the People's Republic of China on Lawyers canceled the regulation that lawyers shall be liable for hiding the truth of facts, the new regulation on confidentiality is still abstract as are the general regulations. For example, the laws don't say anything about information provided to the lawyer by a prospective client or a former client. Also, unlike the U.S.'s Model Rules promulgated by the ABA, which provide that lawyers in a firm may, in the course of the firm's practice, disclose to each other information relating to a client of the firm, unless the client has instructed that particular information be confined to specified lawyers,[19] the law in China does not yet regulate whether or not a lawyer can disclose a client's information to each other in the law firm.

In the 2004 version of the Code of Conduct,[20] there are four exceptions to the confidentiality of information: to prevent the client from committing a crime which will result in death or substantial bodily harm; to prevent the harm of state benefits; the client authorizes the lawyer to disclose; to establish a defense to a criminal charge or civil claim against the lawyer based upon conduct in which the client was involved. But the latest version has deleted these exceptions. Some legal scholars stated that since it is really hard to explain the exact meaning of "state benefits," these limited exceptions are too limited. New situations will happen and the four limitations cannot meet the requirements every time. The new overall exception is: facts and information regarding a client or other person's preparation or current engagement in crimes that endanger state or public security, or seriously endanger the personal safety or others or their property. But there is still a concern totally contrary to the deletion of the four stated limitations. The basket is now too large—you can put more things in the basket—so that there is a worry that lawyer and client confidentiality cannot be fully protected and lawyers still do not have practicable instructions to balance at which point to disclose a client's confidential information.

---

19 AMERICAN BAR ASS'N, MODEL RULES OF PROFESSIONAL CONDUCT r. 1.6 cmt. 5 (2016).

20 Code of Conduct of Lawyer, 2004, http://www.jincao.com/fa/22/law22.34.htm

Another problem that affects client-lawyer confidentiality is China's lack of related bodies of law, such as attorney-client privilege. Attorney-client privilege regulates the relationship between lawyers and the third party other than the client, such as police, prosecutors, and judges. But in China, no laws that regulate lawyers' conduct regulate attorney-client privilege. However, according to criminal procedure law,[21] everybody who knows the facts has the obligation to testify; as criminal procedure law has a higher legal hierarchy than laws that regulate lawyers' conduct, confidentiality without an attorney-client privilege cannot actually work against the criminal procedure obligation to testify.[22]

There is an important reason that it is difficult to maintain client-lawyer confidentiality: the problem of how hard it is to meet the client individually and privately, as the police many times abuse their authority to intervene in lawyer-client meetings for political reasons and state policies. Here, I want to take Li Zhuang's case as an example. Li Zhuang is a Beijing lawyer who represented Gong Gangmou, an alleged mafia boss in Chong Qing, western China.[23] Li travelled to Chong Qing to interview Gong in jail. According to Criminal Procedure Law, at the trial stage, an attorney can interview the client independently and without the company of the police. But in this case, Li was allowed to interview Gong only if the police accompanied him during his interview.[24] In this way, Li and Gong's attorney-client privilege was obviously violated.[25] Li travelled from Beijing to Chongqing to interview Gong, and he did not expect he would be

---

[21] Criminal procedure law Article 60 provides that everybody who knows the facts of the case has the obligation to testify.

[22] Confidentiality rule of lawyer practice, pp. 14-15, Peipei Bao, China University of Political Science and Law; the article is issued on cnki.net.

[23] Gong was charged with the crime of organizing and leading a criminal syndicate, intentional murder, illegally trading, transporting firearms, and trading and transporting drugs. Li found that these crimes could not be established.

[24] The reason that the jail required a police-accompanied interview was that the state meant to prosecute Gong and other similar criminal offenders as China during that period was fighting against corruption. It was true that Gong is a mafia boss, and his relative has committed a murder crime, and this relative worked with him, but actually the murder case has nothing to do with him. Since the state in truth wanted to make him commit the crimes, the police purposely limited the opportunities for lawyers to investigate the case thoroughly.

[25] Discussion of several questions between attorney and client—from the perspective of "Li Zhuang case," Zhang Dengyin, East China University of Political Science and Law; the article was issued on cnki.net.

deprived of the right to meet his client individually. The situation still requires more specific explanations of law to guarantee lawyer-client confidentiality.

III. Standards for Attorney Fees

In China, lawyers' fees standards can differ according to different geographic areas and subject practice areas. The National Development and Reform Commission and the Ministry of Justice issued the Measures for the Administration of Lawyers' Fees.[26]

According to the Measures, a law firm shall implement government-guided pricing for providing legal services including acting as an agent in civil cases; administrative cases; cases of state compensation; criminal cases, including the providing legal consultancy to, filling complaints and charges for, and applying for probation for criminal suspects; or acting as a defender for the accused, private prosecutor or the victim, and various kinds of litigation cases for appealing to the court. A law firm shall implement market-regulated pricing for providing other legal services.[27] The benchmark price and the floating range of market-regulated price shall be determined by the competent department of price of the people's government of each province, autonomous region, or a municipality directly under the Central Government, together with the judicial administrative department at the same level.[28] The local economic development level, the social affordability, as well as the long-term development of the lawyering industry shall be taken into full account for the government to determine the lawyer's fees. And the charging rates shall be determined on the basis of the social average costs for compensating lawyers' services plus the reasonable profits and statutory taxes.[29]

The lawyers' fees subject to market regulation shall be determined through the consultation between the law firm and the client. When a law firm is consulting about the attorney fees with its clients, time to be spent

---

26 Notice of the National Development and Reform Commission and the Ministry of Justice on Issuing the Measures for the Administration of Lawyers' Fees (No. 611 [2006] of the National Development and Reform Commission), http://www.lawinfo china.com/display.aspx?lib=law&id=5114&CGid=

27 *Id.* Article 5.

28 *Id.* Article 6.

29 *Id.* Article 8.

on the work, complexity of the legal affair, affordability of the clients, risks and responsibilities the law firm might assume, and social reputation and working level, etc. of the lawyers should be taken into account.[30]

The lawyers' fees may, in light of different service contents, be charged on a case-by-case basis,[31] at a certain proportion of the amount involved, or the time spent, etc. The fees charged on a case-by-case basis shall be generally applicable to the legal affairs not involving property relationships. The fees charged on the basis of a proportion of the amount involved shall be applicable to the legal affairs involving property relationships. The fees charged on the basis of the time spent may be applicable to all legal affairs.[32] In the handling of a civil case involving a property relationship, if the client still requires the attorney to implement contingency fees (called in China "risk agency")[33] after being informed of the government-guided pricing, the law firm may charge fees on the basis of risk agency, unless it is under any of the following circumstances: marriage and inheritance case, cases asking for social insurance benefits or minimum subsistence benefits, cases asking for alimony payment, allowance payment, pension, relief fund and employment compensation,[34] or asking for labor remuneration payment.[35] Risk agency charges are not allowed in criminal litigation, administrative litigation, state compensation cases, and class actions.[36] The fee of a risk agency shall not be higher than 30% of the subject matter of the contract amount involved in the claim.[37]

In China, risk agency has long been a highly controversial lawyer charging method. The Chinese lawyer Zhou Litai first started the risk

---

30 *Id.* Article 9.

31 The most popular lawyer charging method in China.

32 *Id.* Article 10.

33 Risk agency is the manner of fee payment much like the lawyer charging a contingency fee in America.

34 This is different from America; in China, the worker's pay compensation suit is banned from risk agency, which makes it more difficult for migrant workers to get their pay back. Employers owing migrant workers pay has been a big social problem in China.

35 *Id.* Article 11.

36 *Id.* Article 12.

37 *Id.* Article 13.

agency in China in 1996. Zhou focused on protecting migrant workers' rights and interests. There have been many migrant workers coming from removal and rural areas to big cities to find opportunities in the past 30 years in China. Employers always delay paying migrant workers' wages, but these workers do not have money to get a lawyer to sue their employers. Zhou realized the problem and first used the risk agency to charge this group of people. Through 2007, he helped more than 7,000 migrant workers to ask for wages from their employers on a risk agency basis. But sadly, because of the lack of regulations and protection to lawyers of risk agency, up to that time, migrant workers have owed him 5,000,000 Yuan (around USD $726,416). Most of the migrant workers got their arrears but did not pay the contingency fee to Zhou as they originally agreed on. Since the National Development and Reform Commission and the Ministry of Justice issued the Measures for the Administration of Lawyers' Fees in 2006, workers' pay compensation is excluded from the risk agency, so that Zhou, as many other lawyers in China who worked for migrant workers, cannot get back the lawyer service fees those migrant workers owed him anymore.[38]

Those workers who left without paying attorney fees may argue that the risk agency is unreasonable. But how to tell reasonableness? In China, there is no law or case talking about this. A U.S. case, *Maynard Steel Casting Co. v. Sheedy*, explained that the focus of the reasonableness inquiry for the contingent fee is not so much tied to the individual hours or efforts spent on a particular case, but rather it encompasses a broader focus. The basic idea behind the use of the contingent fee is that in some tort cases the attorney may get what seems like a windfall, but in other cases the attorney can take the case through a long trial and appeal and get nothing. Sometimes the risk pays off, and sometimes it does not. A broader focus is important when assessing the reasonableness of the contingent fee.[39] This court approved of the *Meyer* court considering,

---

[38] The Analysis of the Risk Representation System, Shi Yuan, Graduate School of Chinese Academy of Social Sciences. The article issue date: April 1, 2014. This article is issued on cnki.net.

[39] Maynard Steel Casting Co. v. Sheedy, 746 N.W.2d 816, 821 (Wis. 2008). In this case, respondent appealed from a judgment requiring him to disgorge $132,800 in attorney fees. Respondent asserted the trial court applied the wrong burden of proof; Maynard Steel Casting Company failed to present any expert testimony as to the reasonableness of respondent's fees; the trial court improperly substituted its opinion as to the reasonableness of a contingent fee agreement; the trial court erred in invalidating a

besides the existence of the contingent fee contract, three factors: only (1) the time and labor involved, (2) the amount of money involved, and (3) the attendant risks involved need to be considered in determine reasonableness.[40]

China is vast in territory and the economic development is unbalanced in various areas. The chart below is an example of a case-by-case basis fee standard to show the big disparity among different areas.[41]

			Beijing	Xinjiang	Guizhou	Guangdong
			Charges (Yuan)			
Case By Case	Criminal Case	Investigation	2,000-15,000	500-2,000	50-500	3,000-30,000
		Litigation	2,000-15,000	1,000-4,000	500-5,000	6,000-50,000
		Trial of First Instance	4,000-45,000	1,500-5,000	1,000-5,000	6,000-60,000
		Self Prosecution			500-5,000	6,000-60,000
	Civil Case	Property (Below 10,000)	10% contract subject matter	5% contract subject matter	5% contract subject matter	3,000-10,000 plus 10% contract subject matter
		Non-property		500-4,000	1,000-2,000	3,000-15,000

In China, very big cities like Beijing, Shanghai, and Guangzhou always have the higher fee standards. This is also true for coastal provinces and states. Inland and mountainous provinces like Xinjiang, Guizhou, and Qinghai provinces always have lower fee standards. Also these areas lack

---

valid contingent fee agreement; and the trial court erred in holding that respondent assumed no risk in representing Maynard Steel.

[40] Meyer v. Michigan Mutual Ins. Co, 609 N.W.2d 167 (Wis. 2000).

[41] National lawyer charges standard, http://www.lawtime.cn/shoufeibiaozhun/. Now, the fee standard is not a compulsory standard in every province; it is more like a reference for lawyers and law firms, as the details will regulate in each law firm and in courts.

lawyer resources and universities and colleges in these areas do not have strong teaching faculties in law schools. The economic benefits draw lawyers to practice in bigger cities and coastal areas and provinces. In inland underdeveloped areas, the State Council of the People's Republic of China allows much lower fee standards as a part of the anti-poverty project.

However, there have been attorney fee standard disputes in America too. In the case *Goldfarb v. Virginia State Bar*, petitioners who unsuccessfully tried to find a lawyer who would perform title examination for less than the fee prescribed in a minimum fee schedule published by the county bar brought an action against the state and county bars for injunctive relief and damages, alleging that the fee schedule and its enforcement mechanism, as applied to fees for legal services relating to residential real estate transactions, constituted price-fixing in violation of the Sherman Act. In this case, petitioners contacted a lawyer who quoted them the precise fee suggested in a minimum-fee schedule published by respondent Fairfax County Bar Association; the lawyer told them that it was his policy to keep his charges in line with the minimum-fee schedule which provided for a fee of 1% of the value of the property involved. Petitioner then tried to find a lawyer who would examine the title for less than the fee fixed by the schedule. They sent letters to 36 other Fairfax County lawyers requesting their fees. Nineteen replied, and none indicated that he would charge less than the rate fixed by the schedule; several stated that they knew of no attorney who would do so. In this case, the Supreme Court held that, given the substantial volume of commerce involved and the inseparability of this particular legal service from the interstate aspects of real estate transactions, interstate commerce had been sufficiently affected.[42] Where, as a matter of law or practical necessity, legal services are an integral part of an interstate transaction, a

---

[42] Goldfarb v. Virginia State Bar, 421 U.S. 773, 785 (1975). The minimum-fee schedule in this case was a list of prices, suggested by the county bar for various basic legal services, such as wills, marriage contracts, and title searches. The enforcement power lay in the hands of the State Bar, which was the administrative agency used by the Supreme Court of Virginia to regulate the legal profession. The State Bar did not compel adherence to this fee schedule, but it had published several reports condoning the practice and had opined that habitual violation of the minimum-fee schedule suggested misconduct on the part of the lawyer.

restraint on those services may substantially affect commerce for Sherman Act purposes.[43]

IV. Lawyer's Statements Outside of Court

According to Article 73 of Code of Conduct of Lawyer, lawyers or law firms should not express statements in public occasions or media to viciously depreciate, defame, or damage the reputation of other lawyers. Developments in the media have brought us convenience and at the same time, provided lawyers another place to "fight" with each other. This Article is very important to regulate lawyers' and law firms' statements outside of the court; there are some representative cases in China that happened in recent years to alert lawyers to pay more attention to their behavior in front of the public and in social media.

The most significant one is the "Li Tianyi case." In this case, Li Tianyi, a famous Chinese singer's son, was arrested for rape in March, 2013. Just before the trial date, both parties' attorneys started to issue large amounts of information related to the case via their blogs, and it seemed to start a "fight" between the two sides online; among the information given were some facts that were confidential. According to Chinese Criminal Procedure Article 274, if the defendant is below 18 years old when he or she is tried, then the trial should be private. But obviously, in this case, the lawyers did not follow the rule in procedure law and in the ethics code. Later, many of the details of Li's early childhood and his bad behaviors were all exposed to the social media and the public. Finally, Li was sentenced to ten years in prison. Many media actors and jurists in China stated that this is the victory of the people's will. Because he is the son of the most famous military singer, and considered a typical spoiled child of a rich father, the public was so angry with the typical young people like Li that when searching on most of the social media, people gave their opinions that Li should be charged heavily. But what is the truth? It seemed that in this case too much information may have been exposed to the public, and the public would not know which assertion is true, and which one is wrong. What is more important, they do not care much about what the law says, as the status of the victim Yang's work and

---

[43] *Id.* The Court thus struck down the mandatory-fee regulations as violating the Sherman Act's protections against antitrust violations.

past experience have also become public: she worked in a bar and her job was to drink with customers and to entertain them. On the day that the incident happened, she voluntarily left the bar with Li and four other males, and went to a hotel with them. There are still many doubts in this case, but what is undoubted is that the public believes Li deserved it. If at the very beginning, lawyers in the case worked more professionally and responsibly, then the trial result could be much fairer. At least, the judge would not bear the burden of meeting the public's expectation. The Beijing Lawyer Association investigated the six lawyers' behavior in the case and decided to give them a denouncement.[44]

Another example is "Yao Jiaxin's case." Yao was a junior student at Xi'an Music College. He hit a woman, Zhang Miao, with his car in October of 2010, after sending his girlfriend back home. Not wanting to be discovered as having been in an accident and fearing a lawsuit by Zhang, Yao got out of his car and stabbed her with a knife six times. Zhang died as a result. People shocked about this incident, and Zhang's family's attorney, all advocated that Yao should be sentenced to the death penalty. During the trial, the Zhang attorney wrote many things about Yao's family and their background. Some of the things are facts but others are not. These facts included Yao's father's and mother's positions, as well as their annual income. He also stated his opinion that Yao should be sentenced to death. He also put Yao's words that "rural areas people are hard to deal with" on the internet. This triggered the public's anger. He also made details of how Yao stabbed the victim and how cruel it was. Finally, the public and the media seemed all to support the death penalty. This 21-year-old received his lethal injection on June 7, 2011.[45] What is interesting is that, after the death penalty was implemented as to Yao, Zhang's attorney's media statements were criticized and some of the statements were found to be not true. But all of this is too late. A young man has gone to another world.

While the Chinese Constitution protects a citizen's freedom of speech, it is appropriate for Code of Conduct of Lawyer to restrict a lawyer's

---

44 *The powerful public statement will determine Li Tianyi's sentence,* http://blog.sina.com.cn/s/blog_5e54397201019qss.html; *Three cases: statement outside the court affects the trail outcome,* http://news.sohu.com/20130905 /n385931207.shtml (both previously available as of March 21, 2017).

45 *China executes student for murder of hit-and-run victim,* BBC NEWS, June 7, 2011, http://www.bbc.com/news/world-asia-pacific-13678179 (last visited June 26, 2017).

statement outside court. However, Article 73 only regulates the lawyer's statement against other lawyers and law firms; this does not include talking about the clients. So there are still no specific regulations about lawyers' outside statements about the case and their clients. This is the reason why the public gets to know so much about "Li Tianyi's case" and "Yao Jiaxin's case."

Media in China play a great role. Though in the early days, there were many restrictions on the freedom of speech in China, now things have been changed. Many media actors in China now are able to report almost everything in China. CCTV, the media controlled by the Communist Party of China, may still have some restrictions about what to report, yet other media outlets now have more freedom and rights to decide what they want to let the public know. The problem is that the media has changed from saying nothing to saying everything, making the situation worse. There are not many laws regulating the speech of media, so, as a result, the media most of the time mislead the public. So when the lawyer talks outside the court and use the media to publicize their speech, things can go wrong. Some lawyers in China hold the opinion that the media help to uphold justice, but from the recent cases like "Li Tianyi" and "Yao Jiaxin," this opinion is wrong. In these cases, the media took upon itself the role of accuser and judge, and these cases were more like a trial by media and the public. While there should be some bright lines about what lawyers can talk about outside the court, and what lawyers cannot say outside the court, media in China should also be regulated in the future.

In an earlier time, a leading case in the United States, *Sheppard v. Maxwell*, identified the need for trial publicity reform and shaped the ABA's remedial measures in the U.S. The Supreme Court admonished the trial court in *Sheppard* for its failure to control the extrajudicial publicity: the fact that many of the prejudicial news items can be traced to the prosecution, as well as the defense, aggravated the judge's failure to take any action. Effective control of these sources—concededly within the court's power—might well have prevented the divulgence of inaccurate information, rumors, and accusations that made up much of the inflammatory publicity.[46] In the ABA's Model Rules, Rules 3.5 and 3.6 are

---

46 Sheppard v. Maxwell, 384 U.S. 333, 360 (1966). The facts of the case are that Sam Sheppard was accused of murdering his wife Marilyn Reese Sheppard, and the murder investigation and the trial were notable for extensive publicity. Some newspapers and other media in Ohio were accused of bias against Sheppard and of inflammatory coverage, and they were criticized for immediately labeling Sheppard as the only viable

very helpful.[47] The "substantial likelihood of material prejudice" standard is a constitutionally permissible balance between the First Amendment rights of attorneys in pending cases and the state's interest in fair trials.[48]

In the case *U.S. v. McGregor*, the court discussed the issue of when a court should issue a gag order. A court should issue a gag order only if: (1) the attorneys' speech presents a substantial likelihood of material prejudice to the proceedings; (2) the proposed protective order is narrowly tailored; (3) alternatives to the protective order would not be effective; and (4) the order would be effective in achieving the government's goal.[49] The U.S. Supreme Court has instructed that gag orders address "two principal evils: (1) comments that are likely to influence the actual outcome of the trial, and (2) comments that are likely to prejudice the jury venire, even if an untainted panel can ultimately be found."[50]

V. Conclusion

Decades ago, when Chinese people had some trouble in their lives, they used to ask people that they are familiar with for help, because of the long history of nepotism society. Things are still the same today, but as

---

suspect. It appeared that the local media did influence investigators. On July 21, 1954, the *Cleveland Press* ran a front-page editorial entitled "Do It Now, Dr. Gerber," which called for a public inquest. Hours later, Dr. Samuel Gerber, the coroner who was investigating murder, announced that he would, the next day, hold an inquest. The *Cleveland Press* ran another front-page editorial on July 30 entitled "Why Isn't Sam Sheppard in Jail?" which was titled in later editions, "Quit Stalling and Bring Him In!" That night, Sheppard was arrested for a police interrogation. *See id.*

47 Rule 3.5: "A lawyer shall not: (a) seek to influence a judge, juror, prospective juror or other official by means prohibited by law; (b) communicate ex parte with such a person during the proceeding unless authorized to do so by law or court order. . . ." Rule 3.6(a): "A lawyer who is participating or has participated in the investigation or litigation of a matter shall not make an extrajudicial statement that the lawyer knows or reasonably should know will be disseminated by means of public communication and will have a substantial likelihood of materially prejudicing an adjudicative proceeding in the matter."

48 *See* Gentile v. State Bar of Nevada, 501 U.S. 1030, 1051-53 (1991).

49 U.S. v. McGregor, 838 F.Supp.2d 1256, 1262 (M.D. Ala. 2012). On the eve of the retrial in this public-corruption case, the government moved for a gag order limiting what the parties' trial teams could state to the media. Rather than adopting the government's proposed gag order, the court required all attorneys to comply with Alabama Rule of Professional Conduct rule 3.6, which provides guidelines for how lawyers should interact with the press during criminal trials.

50 *Gentile*, 501 U.S. at 1075.

more and more start to realize the problem of nepotism society, many people start to find justice and lawyers to help them solve their problems. As discussed above, there are many cases that have happened in recent years in China which engendered hot discussions among lawyers, legal scholars, and the public. People discussed these issues because they never happened before—or they happened but society did not recognize them, or society did not realize the necessity of resolving the issues.

Chairman Xi Jinping has emphasized the importance of using law to govern the country. He hopes that the quality of the legal profession in China can be improved. Several past chairmen in China made their focus on reformation and opening society, and on economic development. Now China has become more and more developed and international, but many social issues have come out at the same time. It is time to give more effort to improvement of the legal system. As Xi emphasizes, Chinese lawyers will be more professional.

Now, more and more people realize the importance of using law to protect their rights, and they make more contacts with lawyers. Law schools at every university are making progress gradually, trying to make the courses more useful and make it easier for students to transition from the role of student to the role of lawyer. And the National Judicial Exam is also under development, which will likely become more professional and only allow law school students to take it.

However, the legal profession in China is still relatively a new profession. In many parts of China, there are still people who do lawyers' work but have never attended a law school. Lawyers in China have recognized the importance of acting ethically, but there have not been enough detailed and specific rules to train and instruct them. Many lawyers reflect that they received training about legal profession ethics rules at work, but that is really superficial training.

As more questions will arise in the near future, lawyer behaviors will be considered by more bar associations, local or state, and by legal scholars and lawyers themselves. Today, big law firms in China have regular, annual legal ethics training; however, lawyers attend the training but do not pay much attention to its importance. We expect that the image of lawyers can be a good one: a client can trust his or her lawyer and the judge. Big law firms set up regulations and rules to train their lawyers and inform them about the new changes and updates to the ethics rules.

This is a very good start and one hopes this is not only a limitation on the behavior of lawyers, but also will help to upgrade the lawyer's image in the whole society. But this seems a challenge in today's China. China already has a crisis of trust in the whole society, and specifically in judicial systems, there are problems like judges who are not independent and even judges who accept bribery from lawyers.

The larger atmosphere is really challenging for every law practitioner. As the legal profession is always a challenging career—all the time, all around the world—what Chinese lawyers struggle with now probably is the same as what other lawyers have gone through. Chinese lawyers are hard-working, dedicated, and passionate, both young and old, man and woman. Though there are trust issues, lawyers have tried to prove themselves. But in the end, what is important is still using rules and regulations to instruct the legal profession, because humans are not perfect and this is so true as to lawyers.

PART THREE

The Legal Profession's Challenges and Future

7

The Cost of Getting Ahead: An Examination of Adderall Abuse, Effects, and Solutions Among Law Schools

Marissa Delgado

> In the hands of the wise, poison is medicine.
> In the hands of a fool, medicine is a poison.
> — Giacomo Casanova (Italian Physician, 1725–1798)

I. Introduction

Alcoholism, drug addiction, and various mental health problems affect many law students, lawyers, and judges. The American Bar Association estimates that only ten percent of the general population battles alcoholism and drug abuse, but anywhere between fifteen and eighteen percent of the legal profession population face the same problems.[1] The ABA argues that this is because many in the legal profession "are overachievers who carry an enormous workload there is the tendency to 'escape' from daily problems using drugs and alcohol."[2] Further, the ABA notes that the pressures placed on legal professionals lead to "inordinate amounts of stress and mental illness."[3] Several recent reports show that most disciplinary problems within the legal field are the results of stress and dependency on alcohol and drugs.[4]

Prescription drug abuse is more prevalent than ever before. There is evidence that prescription drug abuse may overtake the use of illicit

---

[1] American Bar Commission on Lawyer Assistance Programs Association, "Substance Use and Mental Health Toolkit for Law School Students and Those Who Care About Them" (2004). The current version is found in a PDF, which is available at https://www.americanbar.org/content/dam/aba/administrative/lawyer_assistance/ls_colap_mental_health_toolkit_new.authcheckdam.pdf (last accessed June 21, 2017).

[2] *Id.*

[3] *Id.*

[4] *Id.*

drugs.[5] Among law students, the growth of the use of Adderall and similar medications is rising exponentially.[6] The effects of this development can lead to many psychological and physical health issues.[7] This chapter will focus on the history of how the ABA has handled drug addiction among law students, the problems with the Adderall black market among universities, why law students look to Adderall, and various solutions to the problem. This chapter is a call for action among law schools and the ABA to seriously reconsider and expand existing policies on not only Adderall but other forms of substance abuse.

II. The American Bar Association and Chemical Dependency (ABA Toolkit)

A. History of the ABA's Involvement

The American Bar Association in 1988 created the Commission on Impaired Attorneys in order to help aid lawyers whose practices were affected by addictions.[8] In August 1996, the Commission on Impaired Attorneys was renamed to the Commission of Lawyer Assistance Programs (CoLAP).[9] CoLAP was created to expand the Commission's services. These services focused on stress, depression, and other mental health problems.[10] The central goal of CoLAP was to advance knowledge within the legal community about the impairments that face those in the legal profession and the community's response to those issues.[11] The Commission is made up of ten members with five of the members in

---

[5] Jason P. Caplan, et al., *Neuropsychiatric Effects of Prescription Drug Abuse*, 17 NEUROPSYCHOL. REV. 363 (Aug. 16, 2007).

[6] *Id.*

[7] American Bar Commission on Lawyer Assistance Programs Association, "Substance Use and Mental Health Toolkit for Law School Students and Those Who Care About Them" (2004). For the most current version of this helpful guide, see https://www.americanbar.org/content/dam/aba/administrative/lawyer_assistance/ls _colap_mental_health_toolkit_new.authcheckdam.pdf (last accessed June 21, 2017).

[8] *Id.*

[9] *Id.*

[10] *Id.*

[11] *Id.*

recovery from drug abuse and alcoholism.[12] The ABA considers the Commission successful in introducing support programs in state and local bars.[13] Due to the work of the Commission, all fifty states have developed lawyer assistance programs or committees that focus on the quality of life issues that surround the legal profession.[14] These programs or commissions offer intervention, peer counseling, and referral to twelve step programs.[15]

Due to the high occurrences of alcoholism and chemical dependency within the legal profession as well as the implications the problem causes for the legal profession and the public, there are many different organizations that have worked towards affirmatively addressing the issues surrounding substance abuse.[16] In 1988, the ABA's Commission on Impaired Attorneys created a policy for law firms and corporate legal departments to use for personal impairment.[17] This included a handbook, "Guiding Principles for a Lawyer Assistance Program."[18] The ABA House of Delegates has approved changes in response to chemical dependency in the ABA Standards for Imposing Lawyer Sanctions.[19] These changes include "balancing the acknowledged need to protect this public with the need to treat chemical dependency in an enlightened manner as a curable disease."[20] At the state and local levels, lawyer assistance programs (LAPs) help attorneys to address their substance abuse issues.[21]

---

[12] *Id.*

[13] American Bar Association, "Substance Use Disorders and Mental Health Interest Group," http://www.americanbar.org/groups/health_law/interest_groups/educational_outreach/substance_abuse.html (last accessed March 10, 2017).

[14] *Id.*

[15] *Id.*

[16] *Id.*

[17] *Id.*

[18] *See* American Bar Association, "Commission on Lawyer Assistance Programs," http://www.americanbar.org/groups/lawyer_assistance.html (last accessed March 10, 2017). For the "Guiding Principles" handbook downloadable as a PDF, see also https://www.americanbar.org/content/dam/aba/administrative/lawyer_assistance/ls_colap_guiding_principles_for_assistance.authcheckdam.pdf.

[19] American Bar Association, "Commission on Lawyer Assistance Programs," http://www.americanbar.org/groups/lawyer_assistance.html

[20] *Id.*

[21] *Id.*

In the 1990s, The AALS Executive Committee created The Special Committee on Problems of Substance Abuse in Law Schools.[22] The Special Committee examined various problems of substance abuse in the law school setting and developed different recommendations to enhance the various ways in which law schools deal with these problems.[23] The Committee undertook two different surveys to try to obtain current and accurate information about the extent of chemical dependency and substance abuse in law schools.[24] The first survey was conducted on law school administrators, and the second survey was conducted on law students.[25]

Using the information gathered from the surveys, the Committee made several recommendations that were intended to provide both information and advice that would be useful for law schools to develop their approach to chemical dependency.[26] The Committee's report focused on encouraging each law school to "examine its own specific situation and develop an approach to the problems of substance use that is tailored to the unique needs of the individual institution, its students and faculty."[27] In its accompanying Toolkit, the Committee emphasized that the report did not suggest any changes in AALS Requirements of Membership or that member schools should adopt certain policies or programs.[28]

B. The ABA and Law School

In 2002, the Commission created a new Law School Outreach Committee.[29] The Committee was created after The Special Committee of the Association of American Law Schools (AALS) published a report about

---

[22] *See id.*

[23] Rachel G. Packer, "A Young Lawyer's Guide to Ethically Confronting Substance Abuse," American Bar Association, June 7, 2012, http://apps.americanbar.org/litigation/committees/youngadvocate/email/spring2012/spring2012-0612-young-lawyers-guide-ethically-confronting-substance-abuse.html (last accessed June 21, 2017).

[24] *Id.*

[25] *Id.*

[26] *Id.*

[27] *Id.*

[28] *Id. See supra* note 7, linking the current version of the Toolkit.

[29] Robert A. Stein, *Help is Available*, 91 ABA JOURNAL 64 (June 2005).

substance abuse in law schools.[30] In its report, the AALS made several recommendations for law schools to successfully examine and act on the issue of substance abuse by students and faculty.[31] "The Commission believes that in order to be effective, more should be done to reach lawyers at an earlier stage of law school."[32] Thus, in 2003, a group of law school deans, professors, members of the Commission, and other interested parties were brought together to examine the issues and come up with a solution to reach law students. This group developed a Toolkit to assist law schools in this area.[33]

III. Adderall Abuse and Effects

Adderall is a prescription drug conventionally prescribed to treat such conditions as Attention Deficit Hyperactivity Disorder (ADHD), and it is used by many students every day to study for exams. In a survey of 1,387 students, 591 of these students took Adderall without a prescription or a diagnosis of ADHD.[34] Further, approximately 25 percent of college students have admitted to using Adderall to help them prepare for exams.[35] Also, since 1990, Adderall and other ADHD medication sales have increased by 400 percent.[36]

A. What is Adderall?

Adderall is a "single-entity amphetamine product combining the neutral sulfate salts of dextroamphetamine and amphetamine, with the dextro isomer of amphetamine saccaharate and d, I-amphetamine aspartate."[37] It is used mainly to help treat people with ADHD and

---

30 *Id.*

31 *Id.*

32 *Quoted in id.*

33 *Id. See supra* note 7, linking the current version of the Toolkit.

34 Jason P. Caplan, et al., *Neuropsychiatric Effects of Prescription Drug Abuse*, 17 NEUROPSYCHOL. REV. 363 (Aug. 16, 2007).

35 *Id.*

36 *Id.*

37 Drugs.com, "Adderall," http://www.drugs.com/pro/adderal.html (last accessed Feb. 23, 2017).

narcolepsy. Adderall stimulates the production of dopamine and norepinephrine in the brain which increases concentration.[38] When students who do not have ADHD take Adderall, it over-stimulates the brain and thus creates super-enhanced focus.[39]

Adderall is not difficult for students to access. Even to those who do not have a prescription for Adderall, finding the drug is quite simple.[40] Students can look for another person with a prescription who is willing to sell or give away their Adderall pills, thus creating a black market for the drug.[41] In some universities, students can go to their campus's health clinic and obtain a prescription for Adderall after being diagnosed with ADHD. The lax measures then cause many students to be misdiagnosed with ADHD.[42] Recently, students have started selling their Adderall pills illegally to others. Those with the pills not only have the benefit of super-enhanced concentration that benefits their own academic performance, they can earn an income by selling the pills.[43] This also contributes to the creation of an Adderall black market.[44] Adderall is also used for recreational purposes. The same drug that enhances concentration can also be used to get high.[45]

B. Side Effects

Harmful side effects of Adderall usage include insomnia, loss of appetite, hallucinations, seizures, and uncontrolled shaking and body movements.[46] The warning label on Adderall includes "fast, pounding, or un-

---

[38] Jason P. Caplan, et al., *Neuropsychiatric Effects of Prescription Drug Abuse*, 17 NEUROPSYCHOL. REV. 363 (Aug. 16, 2007).

[39] Helia Garrido Hull, *Regression by Unleveling the Classroom Playing Field Through Cosmetic Neurology*, 33 U. HAW. L. REV. 193, 195 (2010).

[40] *Id.*

[41] Jason P. Caplan, et al., *Neuropsychiatric Effects of Prescription Drug Abuse*, 17 NEUROPSYCHOL. REV. 363 (Aug. 16, 2007).

[42] *Id.*

[43] *Id.*

[44] *Id. See also* Drugs.com, "Adderall," http://www.drugs.com/pro/adderal.html (last accessed Feb. 23, 2017).

[45] Jason P. Caplan, et al., *Neuropsychiatric Effects of Prescription Drug Abuse*, 17 NEUROPSYCHOL. REV. 363 (Aug. 16, 2007).

[46] *Id.*

even heartbeat; feeling light-headed, fainting, increased blood pressure (severe headache, blurred vision, trouble concentrating, chest pain, numbness, seizure); or tremor, restlessness, hallucinations, unusual behavior, or motor tics (muscle twitches)."[47] These side effects are even more drastic for those who do not have ADHD. When Adderall is misused, over time severe psychological issues and physical dependence can occur. Adderall is considered a Schedule II drug by the United States Drug Enforcement Administration (DEA).[48] This indicates that there is a high potential for abuse. By using Adderall without a prescription, there is a higher probability of experiencing the negative side effects and developing a substance abuse problem.[49]

IV. Why Adderall in the Legal Field is an Issue

Substance abuse in American law schools is a problem and deserves the attention of legal educators because it later affects the quality of the legal profession and the services of attorneys who can become impaired due to chemical dependency.[50] The beginning of many drug abuse issues starts during law school years.[51] Patterns of misuse have suggested that law students are developing various behaviors that will be problematic in their professional careers later own.[52] These behaviors include a chemical dependency to relax or relieve tension and as a way to "get away from problems."[53] Further, alcoholism and other chemical dependencies are a progressive disease that will get worse if not treated.[54]

---

47 *Id.*

48 *Id.*

49 *Id.*

50 American Bar Commission on Lawyer Assistance Programs Association, "Substance Use and Mental Health Toolkit for Law School Students and Those Who Care About Them" (2004). For the current version, see https://www.americanbar.org/content/dam/aba/administrative/lawyer_assistance/ls_colap_mental_health_toolkit_new.authcheckdam.pdf (last accessed June 21, 2017).

51 *Id.*

52 *Id.*

53 *Id.*

54 Leigh Jones, *Adderall in Law Schools: A Dirty Little Secret*, Law.com, Nov. 3, 2016, http://www.law.com/sites/almstaff/2016/11/03/adderall-in-law-schools-a-dirty-little-secret/ (last accessed June 28, 2017).

Chemical dependency is a significant problem in many professions and the general citizenry.[55] There are several nationwide reports from lawyer assistance programs (LAPs) that show that anywhere between 50 to 75 percent of attorney disciplinary cases involve chemical dependency or substance abuse.[56] For example, a study conducted by the Washington State Bar Association reported that about 18 percent of lawyers that practiced in the state were alcohol dependent.[57] Further, the medical profession also deals with similar issues of chemical dependency.[58] There was a study done of U.S. medical school students that indicated a significantly higher level of substance abuse by fourth-year medical students than people their own age with college degrees.[59]

These trends raise several questions including, "What is the situation in law schools?"[60] When the Committee surveyed American law school students, 81 percent had used alcohol, 8.2 percent had used marijuana, and 8.8 percent had used another illicit drug all within the last 30 days.[61] This 30-day test is thought in the scientific community to be a valid predictor of regular usage.[62] The Committee compared the results of law students to college and high school graduates of their same age and found that law students had a higher result of regular abuse of alcohol and

---

[55] *Id.*

[56] *Id.*

[57] *Id.*

[58] *Id.*

[59] American Bar Commission on Lawyer Assistance Programs Association, "Substance Use and Mental Health Toolkit for Law School Students and Those Who Care About Them" (2004). *See supra* note 7, linking the current version of the Toolkit. *See generally* American Bar Comm'n on Lawyer Assist. Programs Ass'n, "Toolkit History and Sources: Substance Use and Mental Health Toolkit for Law School Students and Those Who Care About Them" (earlier version providing background to issue, and noting issues with medical students and programs to address abuse there), https://www.americanbar.org/content/dam/aba/administrative/lawyer_assistance/ls_colap_toolkit_history_and_sources.authcheckdam.pdf (last accessed June 28, 2017).

[60] *See* sources cited *supra*, note 59. For example, the "Toolkit History and Sources" paper notes: "The prevalence of substance use in medical schools and the medical profession raises the question what is the situation in law schools?"

[61] *See* sources cited *supra*, note 59. *See also* Leigh Jones, *Adderall in Law Schools: A Dirty Little Secret*, Law.com, Nov. 3, 2016, http://www.law.com/sites/almstaff/2016/11/03/adderall-in-law-schools-a-dirty-little-secret (last accessed June 28, 2017).

[62] American Bar Commission on Lawyer Assistance Programs Association, "Substance Use and Mental Health Toolkit for Law School Students and Those Who Care About Them" (2004). *See supra* note 7, linking the current version of the Toolkit.

psychedelic drugs.[63] The study showed that the results were like medical students and their abuse was higher than in the general population.[64]

The Committee's Report also pointed out trends among law students that put them at high risks for substance abuse. For example, the abuse of certain substances began before entering law school, and it escalated during the time the student was in law school.[65] Also, the report from the survey indicated that 11.7 percent of the students abused alcohol since enrolling at their law school, 8.2 percent had been using marijuana, and 4 percent were drinking alcohol daily.[66] This means that nationwide, there are as many as 4,900 law students who use alcohol daily, 15,000 law students who have abused alcohol, and over 10,600 who have use marijuana in the past 30 days.[67] These numbers alone should be a major concern among the legal community.[68]

Virtually all law schools have students who are impaired, and these students are at risk of becoming dependent on chemical substances.[69] Therefore, the problem of substance abuse is something that every law school should at least devote some attention to correcting. Specifically, when it comes to Adderall abuse, these trends reflect how illicit drug abuse is common, making it more likely that law students are willing to use Adderall without a prescription.

Although the number of prescriptions for Adderall has remained unchanged among young adults over the years, it is reported that misuse and emergency room visits related to the drug have risen dramatically, according to a study by Johns Hopkins published in the *Journal of*

---

[63] *Id.*

[64] *Id.*

[65] *Id.*

[66] *Id.*

[67] Rachel G. Packer, "A Young Lawyer's Guide to Ethically Confronting Substance Abuse," American Bar Association, June 7, 2012, http://apps.americanbar.org/litigation/committees/youngadvocate/email/spring2012/spring2012-0612-young-lawyers-guide-ethically-confronting-substance-abuse.html (last accessed June 21, 2017).

[68] American Bar Commission on Lawyer Assistance Programs Association, "Substance Use and Mental Health Toolkit for Law School Students and Those Who Care About Them" (2004). For the current version, see https://www.americanbar.org/content/dam/aba/administrative/lawyer_assistance/ls_colap_mental_health_toolkit_new.authcheckdam.pdf (last accessed June 21, 2017).

[69] *Id.*

Clinical Psychiatry.[70] The study also found that the principle source of misuse and emergency room visits related to the drug "was the result of diversion—people taking medication that was legitimately prescribed to someone else."[71]

Yet it is unlikely that using Adderall to improve cognitive performance works for law students.[72] Adderall has a placebo effect in which this improvement is merely perceived and thus makes it difficult for the drug to have a direct effect.[73] According to Dr. Martha Farah at the Center for the Cognitive Neuroscience at the University of Pennsylvania, people taking Adderall without a prescription believe that they are doing better than they are, but there is no improvement and sometimes a worse performance.[74]

Posts by law school students on anonymous blogs and message boards show the extensiveness of the misuse of Adderall among law students.[75] For example, a question on Reddit about the use of Adderall in law school led to a vast number of comments.[76] These comments included, "It's prevalent, it's also hilariously obvious to anyone who has taken it when others are on it," "It seemed like everyone and their brother was taking them at my school," and "I was surprised come finals time how many people were taking Adderall or something similar."[77] Further, *Law.com* tried to contact Yale Law School, Harvard Law School, and Stanford Law School (all considered to be top law schools) about the misuse and abuse of Adderall and other similar drugs, but spokeswomen from Harvard and Yale had no comment.[78] The Stanford spokeswoman

---

70 Leigh Jones, *Adderall in Law Schools: A Dirty Little Secret*, Law.com, Nov. 3, 2016, http://www.law.com/sites/almstaff/2016/11/03/adderall-in-law-schools-a-dirty-little-secret/ (last accessed June 28, 2017).

71 *Id.*

72 Jason P. Caplan, et al., *Neuropsychiatric Effects of Prescription Drug Abuse*, 17 NEUROPSYCHOL. REV. 363 (Aug. 16, 2007).

73 *Id.*

74 Leigh Jones, *Adderall in Law Schools: A Dirty Little Secret*, Law.com, Nov. 3, 2016, http://www.law.com/sites/almstaff/2016/11/03/adderall-in-law-schools-a-dirty-little-secret/ (citing study) (last accessed June 28, 2017).

75 *Id.*

76 *Id.*

77 *Id.*

78 *Id.*

was not aware of any students at Stanford with the problem and that there was nothing else to add.[79]

When it comes to addressing the abuse of Adderall specifically, student abuse has been on the rise for nearly two decades but law schools have not specifically addressed the problem.[80] In one survey and study, the authors believed that one of the reasons why was that law schools did not want to admit illegal drug use was occurring in their law school.[81] Law schools are willing to admit that the abuse is a national but not a local problem.[82]

V. Why Adderall is the Drug of Choice Among Law Students: "It's a Law Student's Steroid"

There are many reasons why law students are now choosing Adderall over other drugs. Most students who admit to using Adderall without the doctor's approval have used the drug because they attribute the drug with not only intensified focus and stimulating the brain but also eliminating the need for sleep or breaks.[83] Legal education creates a stressful and difficult environment because there are only a limited number of exams that determine the students' success in law school (and what inevitably is believed to be their success after law school).[84] In response, law students will turn to Adderall and other drugs in hopes of gaining an edge over other students or to "even out the playing field" if they believe other students are also using Adderall.[85]

The associate academic dean for student life at Texas Tech University College of Law, John Delony, stated, "It's become so normed" and "they're

---

[79] *Id.*

[80] *Id.*

[81] *Id.* (citing "Suffering in Silence: The Survey of Law Student Well-Being...," a survey discussed *infra*, text accompanying note 91).

[82] *Id.*

[83] Jason P. Caplan, et al., *Neuropsychiatric Effects of Prescription Drug Abuse*, 17 NEUROPSYCHOL. REV. 363 (Aug. 16, 2007).*Id.*

[84] Leigh Jones, *Adderall in Law Schools: A Dirty Little Secret*, Law.com, Nov. 3, 2016, http://www.law.com/sites/almstaff/2016/11/03/adderall-in-law-schools-a-dirty-little-secret/ (last accessed June 28, 2017)

[85] *Id.*

hiding it" when he descried the use of Adderall among law students.[86] As one reported noted, "Obtained through friends, friends of friends or family, Adderall taken without a prescription—and law schools' disinclination to address the problem—has created a dirty little secret on campuses across the country, where students, ironically, are breaking the law in order to become lawyers."[87] Law school students generally view Adderall as a harmless study drug.[88] These students do not realize that improvement in their performance is doubtful when using Adderall illegally.[89] They are not aware of the fact that mental health professionals and educators warn that law students' reliance on Adderall imperils their health as well as making them ill-prepared to handle the pressures and challenges that are an integral part of the legal profession.[90]

In "Suffering in Silence," a recent survey conducted by legal educators of 3,400 law students, the authors showed that 14 percent of the respondents had taken a prescribed drug without a prescription within the past year, and that of those students, 79 percent stated that Adderall was the stimulant they took without the prescription.[91] Students pointed out that the reasons for taking Adderall and stimulant drugs like it were enhanced academic performance, better concentration, the ability to study longer, and an increase in alertness.[92]

Dean John Delony believes that the number of law students taking Adderall without a prescription is probably a lot higher but students are reluctant to share information about their use of Adderall because they fear that it would jeopardize their standing within the law school and the admission to the bar.[93] When describing the use of Adderall in his law

---

[86] *Quoted in id.*

[87] *Id.*

[88] *Id.*

[89] *Id.*

[90] *Id.*

[91] Jerome M. Organ, David B. Jaffe & Katherine M. Bender, *Suffering in Silence: The Survey of Law Student Well-Being and the Reluctance of Law Students to Seek Help for Substance Use and Mental Health Concerns*, 66 J. LEGAL EDUC. 116 (2016).

[92] *Id.*

[93] *See* Leigh Jones, *Adderall in Law Schools: A Dirty Little Secret*, Law.com, Nov. 3, 2016, http://www.law.com/sites/almstaff/2016/11/03/adderall-in-law-schools-a-dirty-little-secret/ (quoting Delony) (last accessed June 28, 2017).

school, a Brooklyn Law School graduate said, "I'd say it's prevalent . . . a fair number of people did not take it."[94] This law student was diagnosed with ADHD in second grade and, while in law school, would share his medication with his friends to help them compete.[95] He admitted to sharing his medication a few times and that by sharing it was "almost kind of helping a friend out. 'Hey, you have a lot of work to do, I have a couple extra.'"[96]

A user on Reddit described the motivation of other students to take Adderall. "It seems great at first, like a secret weapon. But grad/law schools put more work on you than you can possibly accomplish. They do this intentionally. To see how far they can push you. It's a high-pressure, competitive environment that generates collective anxiety everyone seems to buy into. Adderall helps you put the pressure on yourself. It gives an artificial edge. And it promotes anxiety, especially work-related anxiety."[97] This user was not alone in reporting the temptation to take Adderall without a prescription. There were many others on the site who spoke about their struggles with addiction and their frustrations of ending their own cycle of abuse.[98]

Will Meyerhofer, a New York University School of Law graduate who is now a psychotherapist in New York, has noted that Adderall has become so popular because of the feeling of intense focus that it provides.[99] A vast majority of Meyerhofer's clients are attorneys who suffer from Adderall abuse. Meyerhofer has stated that Adderall pills "are magical pills but you take enough and you'll be cleaning the bathroom with a toothbrush."[100] Further, he has reasoned that law school is an ideal environment for Adderall abuse because of the demand of heavy

---

94 *Id.*

95 *Id.*

96 *Id.*

97 *See* Jerome M. Organ, David B. Jaffe & Katherine M. Bender, *Suffering in Silence: The Survey of Law Student Well-Being and the Reluctance of Law Students to Seek Help for Substance Use and Mental Health Concerns*, 66 J. LEGAL EDUC. 116 (2016).

98 Leigh Jones, *Adderall in Law Schools: A Dirty Little Secret*, Law.com, Nov. 3, 2016, http://www.law.com/sites/almstaff/2016/11/03/adderall-in-law-schools-a-dirty-little-secret/ (last accessed June 28, 2017).

99 *Id.*

100 *Quoted in id.*

coursework, "make it or break it" finals, the curve, and class rankings.[101] These are in addition to the fact that the law school environment is "extremely competitive, you're paying all this money for law school, and if you can get a little advantage, it's a recipe for Adderall."[102] Meyerhofer has studied Adderall abuse because it continues in the firms.[103]

VI. Solutions to this Issue

A. Making it Difficult to Obtain a Prescription

ADHD diagnosis is an implication that the existence of the disability has been present before the individual was seven years old.[104] There must be an impairment that has existed in two or more different environments.[105] These environments include social, academic, or employment settings. The problems in concentration must be the result of a mental disorder.[106] In order to diagnosis adults, there needs to be problems with inattentiveness, hyperactivity, mood instability, irritability, temper, impaired stress tolerance, disorganization, and impulsivity.[107] There are an increasing number of adults that are diagnosed with ADHD every day.[108] There is a balance between whether these adults are average-functioning adults who just exhibit some of the behaviors like ADHD or if they have the disability.[109] Recent statistics show that between five and eight percent of children and two to four percent of adults have ADHD.[110] Unfortunately, a much higher percentage of adults are diagnosed and currently taking Adderall.[111] This is the result of there being no current diagnostic criteria

---

101 *Id.*

102 *Quoted in id.*

103 *Id.*

104 Jason P. Caplan, et al., *Neuropsychiatric Effects of Prescription Drug Abuse*, 17 NEUROPSYCHOL. REV. 363 (Aug. 16, 2007).

105 *Id.*

106 *Id.*

107 *Id.*

108 *Id.*

109 *Id.*

110 *Id.*

111 *Id.*

for ADHD in adults. Many students can manipulate the tests and obtain a prescription for Adderall. It has been noted that "this over-prescription of Adderall has been the primary driving force of the black market for the drug."[112]

To combat this issue, the testing for ADHD should become more stringent.[113] This includes prohibiting university health clinics from diagnosing students with ADHD or prescribing Adderall, especially for graduate and professional students.[114] Law schools should require students to seek out a psychiatrist off campus.[115] This should discourage students from faking an ADHD diagnosis as well as leading to a misdiagnosis of the disorder.[116] Because the reality is that misdiagnosis of Adderall will most likely never stop completely, the ABA and law schools should also examine regulating those who use the drug without a prescription.[117]

B. Lawyer Assistance Programs (LAPs) Should be Adapted to a Law School Setting

LAPs can exist in many forms but they all focus on education, diagnosis, intervention, treatment, and assistance in recovery. LAPs could be a way to help provide law students and law faculty the help they need as well as serve as a way for law schools to develop different recovery programs.[118] A major part of LAPs is demonstrating that one of the most effective ways to deal with chemical dependency and substance abuse is to encourage the ability for each student to be seen as an individual case with a unique response in the form of a diagnosis, intervention, treat-

---

112 *Id.*

113 *Id.*

114 *Id.*

115 Leigh Jones, *Adderall in Law Schools: A Dirty Little Secret*, Law.com, Nov. 3, 2016, http://www.law.com/sites/almstaff/2016/11/03/adderall-in-law-schools-a-dirty-little-secret/ (last accessed June 28, 2017).

116 *Id.*

117 *Id.*

118 American Bar Commission on Lawyer Assistance Programs Association, "Substance Use and Mental Health Toolkit for Law School Students and Those Who Care About Them" (2004). For the current version, see https://www.americanbar.org/content/dam/aba/administrative/lawyer_assistance/ls_colap_mental_health_toolkit_new.authcheckdam.pdf (last accessed June 21, 2017).

ment, and aftercare that is needed to help with recovery.[119] These programs would create confidentiality in the program and help grant immunity to those participating in the interventions.[120] Further, LAPs could have a defined role in the disciplinary process and continue in after-care monitoring for sobriety.[121] Law schools could create a LAP that focuses specifically on the abuse of Adderall.[122]

Furthermore, this system has been proven to work among medical colleges that have tried to create various initiatives against substance abuse.[123] These medical schools have adopted Aid for Impaired Medical Students (AIMS) programs. AIMS is considered by experts to be an aggressive program that specializes in early detection, confidentiality, and protection of patients from harm.[124] Confidentiality is a huge bonus to this program because this assures that recovering students can "continue their medical education without stigma or penalty. . . . The ultimate objective is to return the student to a successful professional career."[125]

C. Confidentiality

Confidentiality is an essential part of the programs that would serve law students just like it is in programs designed for lawyers.[126] Medical schools and the bar can teach law schools the need for confidentiality in substance abuse programs.[127] There are conflicting policy considerations

---

[119] Id.

[120] Id.

[121] Id.

[122] Id.

[123] Jason P. Caplan, et al., *Neuropsychiatric Effects of Prescription Drug Abuse*, 17 NEUROPSYCHOL. REV. 363 (Aug. 16, 2007).

[124] See id.

[125] American Bar Commission on Lawyer Assistance Programs Association, "Toolkit History and Sources: Substance Use and Mental Health Toolkit for Law School Students and Those Who Care About Them," https://www.americanbar.org/content/dam/aba/administrative/lawyer_assistance/ls_colap_toolkit_history_and_sources.a uthcheckdam.pdf (last accessed June 28, 2017).

[126] See id., and the Toolkit's current version cited *supra* note 7.

[127] Rachel G. Packer, "A Young Lawyer's Guide to Ethically Confronting Substance Abuse," American Bar Association, June 7, 2012, http://apps.americanbar.org/litigation/committees/youngadvocate/email/spring2012/spring2012-0612-young-

between the need to protect the public from impaired lawyers and the need to encourage attorneys to seek out treatment.[128] Students are concerned that their past substance abuse and current treatment will affect their admission to the bar.[129] There are differing standards between bar admission authorities; law school administrators find it difficult to give students answers to their various concerns about recovery programs.[130] A conflict of interest may exist because the law school administration serves as both a counselor to the students and as an agency that reports to the bar.[131]

One way confidentiality could be assured is by designating counselors that are covered under existing evidentiary privileges. Unfortunately, these privileges only offer limited protection.[132] Thus, a critical safeguard that should be put in place is the ability for the bar admission authorities to give sufficient assurances.[133] A confidential counselor would create more of an incentive for law students to seek help from substance abuse programs.[134]

Unfortunately, it is unlikely that bar admission authorities will agree to stop their inquiry into an applicant's use of illegal substances or the student's treatment for abuse of illegal substances.[135] A student should not be prevented or unduly delayed from being admitted to the bar and the information about the student's abuse and recovery should not be publicized widely to the public.[136] Therefore, the best solution would be for law schools to receive assurances from the bar admission authorities that would still be sufficient to incentivize law school students to seek

---

lawyers-guide-ethically-confronting-substance-abuse.html (last accessed June 21, 2017).

[128] *Id.*

[129] *Id.*

[130] *Id.*

[131] *Id.*

[132] *Id.*

[133] *Id.*

[134] *Id.*

[135] *Id.*

[136] ABA, "Substance Use Disorders and Mental Health Interest Group," http://www.americanbar.org/groups/health_law/interest_groups/educational_outreach/substance_abuse.html (last accessed March 10, 2017).

counseling and treatment.[137] Many states in fact have made these commitments.[138]

D. Expanding Existing Law School Policies on Substance Abuse

Most law schools affiliated with universities have some type of substance abuse policy; however, only a small number of law schools have programs that are specifically tailored for the unique problems that law schools create.[139] Programs that are already in place in law schools include education, counseling, and treatment.[140] "Twenty-five percent of reporting law schools include substance use education in their first-year orientation programs or sponsor substance use presentations."[141] An even smaller number of law schools include substance abuse problems in the Professional Responsibility course.[142]

Law schools should do more preventive education measures. Many university substance abuse programs and policies refer law students to other parts of the campus for counseling and treatment.[143] A "1989 report of the N.Y.U. Senate Commission on the Use and Abuse of Alcohol and Other Drugs Among Students stresses the need for decentralization of university counseling and treatment services, some students would probably prefer to obtain counseling off campus (or at least outside the law school) to reduce the likelihood of detection by their peers."[144] Law

---

[137] *Id.*

[138] *Id.*

[139] *Id.*

[140] *Id.*

[141] *Id.*

[142] *Id. See also* Leigh Jones, *Adderall in Law Schools: A Dirty Little Secret*, Law.com, Nov. 3, 2016, http://www.law.com/sites/almstaff/2016/11/03/adderall-in-law-schools-a-dirty-little-secret/ (last accessed June 28, 2017).

[143] ABA, "Substance Use Disorders and Mental Health Interest Group," http://www.americanbar.org/groups/health_law/interest_groups/educational_outreach/substance_abuse.html (last accessed March 10, 2017).

[144] American Bar Commission on Lawyer Assistance Programs Association, "Toolkit History and Sources: Substance Use and Mental Health Toolkit for Law School Students and Those Who Care About Them," https://www.americanbar.org/content/dam/aba/administrative/lawyer_assistance/ls_colap_toolkit_history_and_sources.authcheckdam.pdf (last accessed June 28, 2017).

schools should examine their school's counseling and treatment program, and that information can then be used within the context and resources of the specific institution.[145]

Also, the ABA Toolkit in Substance Abuse Prevention took the time to address the confidentiality issues within substance abuse programs.[146] "The most disappointing aspect of the policies surveyed is that a large number say absolutely nothing about confidentiality of counseling or treatment."[147] The Committee insisted that law schools try to create an accurate description to the extent of confidentiality requirements in substance abuse programs in their specific jurisdiction.[148] The Committee highlighted what the law school should focus on within their substance abuse policy is the position taken by state bar admission authorities in the use of information regarding substance abuse treatment.[149] The Committee found within their survey that two-thirds of law school students did not know whether their school offered substance abuse programs.[150] The Committee stated, "Clearly, schools having substance use programs must do a better job of informing law students that help [is] available."[151]

A large part of the problem with not only abuse of Adderall among law students, but substance abuse in general, is the fact that law schools have responded inconsistently to the problem.[152] Law schools need to do

---

[145] ABA, "Substance Use Disorders and Mental Health Interest Group," http://www.americanbar.org/groups/health_law/interest_groups/educational_outreach/substance_abuse.html (last accessed March 10, 2017).

[146] *See id.* (discussing Toolkit).

[147] *Id.*

[148] *Id.*

[149] Rachel G. Packer, "A Young Lawyer's Guide to Ethically Confronting Substance Abuse," American Bar Association, June 7, 2012, http://apps.americanbar.org/litigation/committees/youngadvocate/email/spring2012/spring2012-0612-young-lawyers-guide-ethically-confronting-substance-abuse.html (last accessed June 21, 2017).

[150] *Id.*

[151] American Bar Commission on Lawyer Assistance Programs Association, "Toolkit History and Sources: Substance Use and Mental Health Toolkit for Law School Students and Those Who Care About Them," https://www.americanbar.org/content/dam/aba/administrative/lawyer_assistance/ls_colap_toolkit_history_and_sources.authcheckdam.pdf (last accessed June 28, 2017).

[152] Rachel G. Packer, "A Young Lawyer's Guide to Ethically Confronting Substance Abuse," American Bar Association, June 7, 2012, http://apps.americanbar.org/litigation/committees/youngadvocate/email/spring2012/spring2012-0612-young-

more for their students to help combat this problem. They should follow the lead of the bar, the health care profession, and medical schools by being more aggressive towards the issue.[153] By notifying their students of the policies within their jurisdiction, educating students about how to properly handle stress and the long-term effects of drug abuse, and efficiently informing students about various programs that they have in place, law schools could take a major part in helping reduce the issues surrounded by not only Adderall abuse but also the use of other illicit substances in their schools.[154]

As a side note, the Committee also examined substance abuse problems among law school faculty members.[155] The Committee's survey revealed that law school faculty are prone to use illicit drugs like law students.[156] Even though a major portion of law schools or their affiliated universities have created a faculty substance abuse policy, most such programs do not follow through with the faculty member and normally let the situation resolve itself.[157] This trend is viewed as a direct opposition to the medical opinion about what is the appropriate action to resolve such behavior.[158] Instead, the law schools should work towards helping their faculty members to admit and identify their problems, creating interventions and insisting on the correct treatment for the faculty member.[159] This would be effective in helping the faculty member.

The Committee noted that its surveys indicate that law schools are willing to take a proactive stance.[160] Law schools need to create programs that deal with faculty substance abuse problems.[161] Law schools should

---

lawyers-guide-ethically-confronting-substance-abuse.html (last accessed June 21, 2017).

[153] *Id.*

[154] ABA, "Substance Use Disorders and Mental Health Interest Group," http://www.americanbar.org/groups/health_law/interest_groups/educational_outreach/substance_abuse.html (last accessed March 10, 2017).

[155] *Id.*

[156] *Id.*

[157] *Id.*

[158] *Id.*

[159] *Id.*

[160] *Id.*

[161] *Id.*

look towards creating models that include a clearly communicated policy. Various provisions in this policy should allow for leave when the faculty member is seeking treatment as well as heath care or an insurance plan that would allow for extended treatment when there is an issue.[162] The law schools should also choose to cooperate and work closely with local LAPs that would provide further assistance to the faculty member.[163]

Therefore, law schools and their affiliated universities should create a written policy that specifically deals with Adderall abuse and other illicit drugs by their faculty members.[164] Faculty members should be regularly informed about their law school's policy regarding the abuse.[165] The law schools should also have a contingency plan for dealing with faculty members who have become impaired.[166] The policy should include an education program that would inform faculty and staff members about warning signs of illicit substance abuse. This would help faculty, students, and their peers by allowing for early intervention.[167] Law schools should work towards providing early and informal interventions for their faculty and staff.[168] Finally, disciplinary action should be a last resort and should be used as a way to ensure that the afflicted faculty member will participate in treatment programs designed for the specific issue or with a lawyer assistance program.[169]

E. Honor Code

In theory, law schools could address the problem of student substance abuse through their honor code systems.[170] In most law schools, the use of Adderall without a prescription would violate their law school honor

---

[162] *Id.*

[163] *Id.*

[164] *Id.*

[165] *Id.*

[166] *Id.*

[167] *Id.*

[168] *Id.*

[169] *Id.*

[170] Leigh Jones, *Adderall in Law Schools: A Dirty Little Secret*, Law.com, Nov. 3, 2016, http://www.law.com/sites/almstaff/2016/11/03/adderall-in-law-schools-a-dirty-little-secret/ (last accessed June 28, 2017).

code.[171] This is because most honor codes prohibit the violation of school rules and state and federal laws.[172] These codes further require their students who witness violations of the code to tell the school administration.[173] Proponents of this solution argue that taking Adderall without a prescription could also constitute cheating since Adderall could give the user an unfair advantage.[174]

Using the honor code to stop the misuse of Adderall is both cumbersome and ineffective. It would be hard to prove that there was an unfair advantage or that a crime had occurred. Not only would this be costly, it could also be time-consuming.[175] Further, even if the conditions of a violation were met, it would do little to help solve the underlying issues with abuse and addiction.[176]

Even the warning message about the violation of the honor code and the illegality of the use of Adderall without a prescription would do little about the problem.[177] One of the writers of the "Suffering in Silence" survey stated, "We're trying to communicate that we care about you as a student. If the message comes out we're headhunting, then we're definitely driving the students underground. You risk turning students off from getting help."[178] As to the Brooklyn Law Student mentioned earlier, the threat of the honor code would not work: "I really don't think it would have much of an effect, to be honest."[179]

---

[171] *Id.*

[172] *Id.*

[173] *Id.*

[174] *Id.*

[175] *Id.*

[176] *Id.*

[177] *Id.*

[178] *Quoted in* Rachel G. Packer, "A Young Lawyer's Guide to Ethically Confronting Substance Abuse," American Bar Association, June 7, 2012, http://apps.americanbar.org/litigation/committees/youngadvocate/email/spring2012/spring2012-0612-young-lawyers-guide-ethically-confronting-substance-abuse.html (last accessed June 21, 2017).

[179] *Quoted in* Leigh Jones, *Adderall in Law Schools: A Dirty Little Secret*, Law.com, November 3, 2016, http://www.law.com/sites/almstaff/2016/11/03/adderall-in-law-schools-a-dirty-little-secret/ (last accessed June 28, 2017).

F. Other Recommendations

When creating law school programs for law students, law schools should create their own written policy even if the school they are affiliated with has a substance use policy. Law schools should also designate one person who should be a substance abuse coordinator, and the school should publicize that person and encourage people to seek that person out.[180] Law schools should also create educations programs that would enlighten students about the consequences and the treatment of substance abuse.[181] Schools should also consider a general wellness program that would help students release excess stress in a positive manner.

Law schools should also be ready to establish early intervention procedures for their students before the problem escalates. After interventions, law schools should require a medical evaluation and advise law students about treatments and counseling options that are available to them.[182] Law schools should also research the adoption of an alcohol policy,[183] and they should also reach out more to local organizations and coordinate with lawyer assistance programs.[184]

When it comes to disciplining law students about their substance abuse problems, law school sanctions should be consistent with a disease model that emphasizes counseling and treatment over other forms of discipline.[185] Law schools should publicize their programs offered to faculty members, staff, and law students. Law schools should review the Americans with Disabilities Act (ADA) to safeguard the school's policies and practices within the requirements of the act, to ensure that they are

---

[180] Rachel G. Packer, "A Young Lawyer's Guide to Ethically Confronting Substance Abuse," American Bar Association, June 7, 2012, http://apps.americanbar.org/litigation/committees/youngadvocate/email/spring2012/spring2012-0612-young-lawyers-guide-ethically-confronting-substance-abuse.html (last accessed June 21, 2017).

[181] *Id.*

[182] *Id.*

[183] *Id.*

[184] American Bar Commission on Lawyer Assistance Programs Association, "Substance Use and Mental Health Toolkit for Law School Students and Those Who Care About Them" (2004). For the current version, see https://www.americanbar.org/content/dam/aba/administrative/lawyer_assistance/ls_colap_mental_health_toolkit_new.aut hcheckdam.pdf (last accessed June 21, 2017).

[185] *Id.*

not hindering students with ADHD or ADD. This would also protect students with the substance abuse problems because alcoholism and drug affliction are both covered as disabilities under the ADA.[186]

Law schools should also attempt to encourage the state bar admission authorities to (1) maintain confidentiality of the substance abuse information that was revealed to them, (2) restrict the examinations about substance abuse and treatments that students take to only recent events, and (3) allow for qualified applicants that are in the process of recovering from substance abuse programs to be admitted to the bar (even if on a probationary status).[187]

The Association of American Law Schools (AALS) should try to work with the American Bar Association Section of Legal Education and Admissions to the Bar and the National Conference of Bar Examiners. The AALS should also urge various admissions authorities to guarantee admission to practice for what would have been otherwise-qualified applicants who are recovering from substance abuse.[188] Law schools should also make steps toward informing students about the various substance abuse policies of the jurisdictions where their graduates most regularly apply.

Law schools should also establish mindfulness programs and seminars as well as student activities, for-credit classes, and guest speakers (including law school faculty, staff, successful attorneys, and judges) to speak to students about healthy living and how to balance work life. Many law schools have created mindfulness programs including the University of California, Berkeley, School of Law; Harvard Law School; University of Virginia School of Law; University of Florida Levin College of Law; and University of San Francisco School of Law.[189] These programs can be used to drive the point home that abusing Adderall is not a viable strategy, even if such a message is indirect.

Finally, law schools should seriously look at the environment they are creating for their students. The high-stakes and high-pressure feelings of

---

[186] *Id.*

[187] *Id.*

[188] *Id.*

[189] *Id.*

traditional legal education, law students believe, have led them to seek out harmful and illegal ways to deal with this environment.[190]

VII. Conclusion

What is most important for law schools is to admit that Adderall abuse is not just a national problem but a local problem as well. Adderall does provide medical benefits for those with ADHD and thus should not be banned from use by students. In fact, Adderall abuse is dangerous and has serious consequences.[191] Adderall abuse is on the rise, especially among law students, and there needs to be serious actions by law schools and the ABA to combat this problem.[192] Both should reexamine their policies and work with health care professionals to provide intervention and recovery programs. Further, law students should not be afraid of the repercussions of seeking out help. To encourage assistance, there needs to be a guarantee of confidentiality to law school students and law schools. By working towards creating programs that educate law students about the problems of Adderall abuse as well as treatments that help afflicted students, there are many solutions that can help solve this issue.

---

[190] *Id.*

[191] Leigh Jones, *Adderall in Law Schools: A Dirty Little Secret*, Law.com, Nov. 3, 2016, http://www.law.com/sites/almstaff/2016/11/03/adderall-in-law-schools-a-dirty-little-secret/ (last accessed June 28, 2017).

[192] *Id.*

8

The Binary Barrister:
A Review of Increased Automation in Legal Practice

Vincent Yadgood

I. Introduction

In 2014 an IT student from the United Kingdom, 18-year-old Joshua Browder, passed his driving test and shortly thereafter was welcomed to the world of licensed motorists with over 30 traffic tickets.[1] Understandably, Browder struck back: the teenager created "donotpay.co.uk," and what was heralded as the "world's first robot lawyer" was born.[2] In just four months the program was used by 86,000 people to appeal parking fines resulting in a success rate of nearly 40% of appeals leading to fines being overturned.[3] This translated to over £2 million being saved by British motorists.[4] The program was easy to use, and worked by asking users a series of questions such as "were you or someone you know driving?" and determined if "an appeal is justified" and would generate a letter that could be used to appeal the ticket.[5] By June 2016 the chatbot lawyer service, now dubbed "DoNotPay" had taken on 250,000 tickets and successfully appealed 160,000, overturning approximately $4 million in USD.[6] As can be expected Browder and DoNotPay made the news, and it came to my attention while I was browsing Reddit, specifically the R/law subreddit where users met the news with what is best described as

---

[1] Alexander Sehmer, *A teenager has saved motorists over £2 million by creating a website to appeal parking fines,* BUSINESS INSIDER (December 30, 2015, 4:34 AM), http://www.businessinsider.com/joshua-browder-saves-motorists-2-million-with-parking-appeal-website-2015-12 (last visited June 26, 2017).

[2] Anthony Cuthbertson, *Robot lawyer overturns $4 million in parking tickets,* NEWSWEEK (June 29, 2016, 6:42 AM), http://www.newsweek.com/robot-lawyer-chatbor-donotpay-parking-tickets-475751 (last visited June 26, 2017).

[3] Sehmer, *supra* note 1.

[4] *Id.*

[5] Cuthbertson, *supra* note 2.

[6] *Id.*

skepticism.[7] But the impact that automation or the more general advance of technology may have on the practice of law should be of interest to anyone within the legal community.

It has long been understood, or at least assumed, that law is a field that will never lose out to automation as it requires what is commonly referred to as "the human element." But this logic was also adopted by those in medicine and finance, other "white collar" fields where automation was a fantasy, and yet these professions are also seeing a rise in the presence and involvement of automation or artificial intelligence. Which leads us to the question: could the practice of law become automated?

Barring the rise of a dystopian technocracy better suited for science fiction, I find it incredibly unlikely that robots will ever assume the role of full attorneys. But despite the legal profession's aversion to change, technologic advancement marches ever onward, and a degree of automation may already have taken root in the practice of law.

II. Definition

Before the rise of artificial intelligence in the law office can be addressed, we have to determine what "artificial intelligence" (AI) actually means, as the term has been loosely used to refer a variety of different things. When the common person hears artificial intelligence they may think of HAL 9000 from Stanley Kubrick's film *2001: A Space Odyssey*, or one of many other another characters that have been presented as AIs in films, books, or television.[8]

However, in this period of rising technology, the study of artificial intelligence no longer resides in the realm of fiction, but refers to real programs that are far less murderous and far more useful. The study of AI has been more broadly defined by University of California's Stuart Russell as the study of methods for making computers behave intelligently . . . a computer is intelligent to the extent that it does the right thing rather

---

7 IvyGold, *19-Year-Old Programmer Creates DoNotPay, the World's First Robot Lawyer*, REDDIT, https://www.reddit.com/r/law/comments/4e9fqs/19yearold_pro grammer_creates_donotpay_the_worlds/ (last visited June 26, 2017).

8 Jesse Emspak, *What is Artificial Intelligence?*, LIVESCIENCE (June 17, 2016, 10:40 PM), http://www.livescience.com/55089-artificial-intelligence.html (providing several examples of AI in popular culture such as HAL 9000 and Data from *Star Trek*) (last visited June 26, 2017).

than the wrong thing. The right thing is whatever action is most likely to achieve the goal, or, in more technical terms, the action that maximizes expected utility. AI includes tasks such as learning reasoning, planning, perception, language understanding, and robotics.[9]

The term artificial intelligence does not refer to solely to a specific technology or to a specific class of tech, but can be used to encompass the entirety of machines that behave intelligently based off of Russell's definition.[10] For the purposes of this paper, "artificial intelligence" (AI) broadly refers to machines that employ a variety of methods to achieve a specialized goal in an efficient manner.

III. What is the Current Role of AI in the Legal Environment?

Artificial intelligence hasn't only been used to appeal tickets in the UK. AIs have been employed in document drafting, research, and trend recognition in legal offices across the United States. They accomplish these tasks through the application of what is known as branch logic, e-discovery software, and natural language processing. These AI have been employed in ways that indicate a promising future, but the practice of law is slow to change and their application is not as wide spread as it could be, at least compared to other fields. Four methods of intelligent behavior employed by AI in a legal context are examined below.

A. Branch Logic

Despite the blaring of herald trumpets announcing the triumphant arrival of DoNotPay as the first of our new robot overlords, DoNotPay is actually not the first artificial intelligence utilized in a legal capacity. If a primitive AI is considered a "robot lawyer" then robot lawyers have been in use since at least before 2011, when a *Slate* article called attention to the availability of some programs designed for legal practice.[11] The article

---

[9] Stuart Russell, *Q&A: The Future of Artificial Intelligence,* University of California, Berkeley, http://people.eecs.berkeley.edu/~russell/temp/q-and-a.html (last visited June 26, 2017).

[10] *Id.*; Emspak, *supra* note 8.

[11] Farhad Manjoo, *Will Robots Steal Your Job?*, SLATE (September 29, 2011, 2:42 AM), http://www.slate.com/articles/technology/robot_invasion/2011/09/will_robots_steal _your_job_5.html (last visited June 26, 2017).

revealed that several legal tech companies had developed programs to help automate some of the more mundane of legal tasks, like document creation.[12] Fenwick & West, a Silicon Valley law firm, stated that it had adopted some of these "document creation programs" and successfully used them to save their clients time and money.[13]

These programs use branching logic like TurboTax, a program which helps individuals without a large amount of assets do their taxes.[14] Branch logic is best described as a "choose your own adventure" approach to information gathering.[15] The program poses a question and based on the responses pose different questions to lead the respondents through a different route of questioning to gather the relevant information.[16] Coincidentally, DoNotPay employs a similar branching logic to draft appeals letters for its users.[17] The Chief Information Officer of Fenwick & West stated that the use of these programs for certain documents had "reduced the average time we were spending from about 20 to 40 hours of billable time down to a handful of hours. . . . In cases with even extensive documents, we can cut the time of document creation from days and weeks to hours."[18]

B. E-Discovery Software

Another automation to reach the legal front is what has been termed "e-discovery software," which is designed to sift through massive amounts of data. It has been described as "the electronic aspect of identifying, collecting, and producing electronically stored information in response to

---

[12] *Id.*

[13] *Id.*

[14] *Id.*

[15] *Branch Logic*, Qualtrics: Support, https://www.qualtrics.com/support/survey-platform/survey-module/survey-flow/standard-elements/branch-logic/ (last visited June 26, 2017)

[16] *Id.*

[17] Leanna Garfield, *A 19-year-old made a free robot lawyer that has appealed $3 million in parking tickets,* BUSINESS INSIDER (February 18, 2016, 10:17 AM), http://www.businessinsider.com/joshua-browder-bot-for-parking-tickets-2016-2 (last visited June 26, 2017).

[18] Manjoo, *supra* note 11 (internal quotations omitted).

a request for production in a lawsuit or investigation."[19] These programs can use specific keywords or patterns of behavior within the data to find particular pieces of evidence that might be helpful to the case. These programs have been used to sift through e-mail correspondence in civil suits, which could be a horribly time consuming affair for first-year associates.[20] The programs can also be applied to text messages, documents, databases, voicemail, audio and video files, websites, or social media posts—without the need for humans to physically review the information.[21] This can feasibly save a law firm long hours of individual review and research and save the client from being billed for those hours.

C. Natural Language Processing

The *Slate* article from 2011 also mentioned an effort by a startup called Lex Machina to use artificial intelligence to analyze and predict trends based on a database of patent and trademark cases. The database was the most comprehensive collection of patent suits ever assembled, and was collected by a group of attorneys and technologists at Stanford in 2008 under the "Intellectual Property Litigation Clearinghouse."[22] The goal of the database project was to analyze trends in patent litigation through the use of natural language processing and use that data to better assist tech companies in dealing with Patent Monetization Entities.[23]

The method the database project hoped to employ, natural language processing, refers to the ability of a computer program to understand human speech as it is spoken; it is a way for computers to "analyze,

---

[19] *The Basics: What is e-Discovery? (e-Discovery Primer),* Complete Discovery Source, https://cdslegal.com/knowledge/the-basics-what-is-e-discovery/ (last visited June 26, 2017).

[20] Garfield, *supra* note 17.

[21] Complete Discovery Source, *supra* note 19.

[22] *The Lex Machina Story: From Start-up to LexisNexis,* THE ARTIFICIAL LAWYER (March 21, 2017), https://www.artificiallawyer.com/2017/03/21/the-lex-machina-story-from-start-up-to-lexisnexis/ (last visited June 26, 2017).

[23] *Id.* This work is similar to that of Tulane University Law School's Professor Elizabeth Townsend Gard, who has continued to develop Durationator, which is designed to follow the copyright status of a work. *See Durationator Copyright System,* Durationator, http://www.limitedtimes.com/ (last visited June 26, 2017).

understand, and derive meaning from human language."[24] Through the use of natural language processing, developers have created AI that can take large amounts of data and summarize it, translate it, recognize names within it, extract relationships from it, recognize speech, and more. The AI just has to be provided with a source of data.

The aforementioned database project sought to do just that when it became the startup Lex Machina in 2010. It was still in its infancy in 2011 when *Slate* mentioned it as being an exciting idea, but Lex Machina was purchased by LexisNexis in 2015 and was granted access to a much larger database of legal documents for its software to sift through.[25] With a larger amount of data at its disposal, Lex Machina is now used to assist law firms and other companies with finding outside counsel, case assessments, and strategies about when it is an appropriate time to file an "expensive motion."[26] Speaking more objectively, Lex Machina can help a law firm run the numbers on which judges are more likely to be sympathetic, as well as the likelihood of success its strategies may have based on the results of similar cases.[27] Lex Machina also boasts the ability to show companies how much money they are spending for litigation compared to their peers in the industry, what law firms are being used in these cases, and how often.[28]

D. New Multi-Faceted AI

In May 2016 BakerHostetler, a Texas law firm, announced that it would "be the first" to integrate artificial intelligence into its bankruptcy practice.[29] This artificial intelligence is called ROSS, and it uses machine

---

[24] *Introduction to Natural Language Processing (NLP) 2016: Everything You Need to Know About Natural Language Processing,* ALGORITHMIA (August 11, 2016), http://blog.algorithmia.com/introduction-natural-language-processing-nlp/ (last visited June 26, 2017).

[25] *The Lex Machina Story: From Start-up to LexisNexis,* THE ARTIFICIAL LAWYER, *supra* note 22.

[26] Lex Machina, https://lexmachina.com/company/ (last visited June 26, 2017).

[27] Garfield, *supra* note 17.

[28] Lex Machina, *supra* note 26.

[29] Lateral Link, *Biglaw Automation: Whose Job Goes First?,* ABOVE THE LAW (September 9, 2016, 4:31 PM), http://abovethelaw.com/2016/09/biglaw-automation-whose-job-goes-first/?rf=1 (sponsored content at blog) (last visited June 26, 2017).

learning, natural language processing (like Lex Machina), image interpretation, and discourse to aid law firms in finding "relevant resources"—apparently one of the "lowest" levels of work for an associate in a law firm.[30] However, later iterations of ROSS are planned to be capable of performing contract review, drafting, e-discovery and more.[31]

Compared to the earlier AIs, ROSS will apparently be a jack of all trades. ROSS is based off of IBM's "Watson," which is a supercomputer that is famous for answering questions through a combination of artificial intelligence and analytical software.[32] Watson, ROSS's progenitor, has been applied in a multitude of fields and experiments and was met with fascinating successes, including winning the game show *Jeopardy!* in 2011.[33] Remarkably, in 2013, Watson was also purported to have diagnosed cancer better than human doctors.[34] Apparently this success has taken root, as reportedly 90% of nurses that have access to ROSS's predecessor Watson now follow the program's treatment advice.[35] Even though ROSS is in its infancy, the firms that utilize it should see great improvements in efficiency.

IV. What Other Fields Are AIs Being Used In?

Artificial intelligence is being implemented in a number of fields that were previously believed to be "automation proof" as they "required a human touch." Alongside law, fields like finance and medicine are experiencing the integration of AI. While it may be true that the human touch is still absolutely necessary for the total success of a venture, AIs are assuming a much greater role in these professions.

---

[30] *Id.*

[31] *Id.*

[32] Will Knight, *IBM's Watson Is Everywhere—But What Is It?*, MIT TECHNOLOGY REVIEW (October 27, 2016), https://www.technologyreview.com/s/602744/ibms-watson-is-everywhere-but-what-is-it/ (last visited June 26, 2017).

[33] *Id.*

[34] Ian Steadman, *IBM's Watson is better at diagnosing cancer than human doctors*, WIRED (February 11, 2013), http://www.wired.co.uk/article/ibm-watson-medical-doctor (last visited June 26, 2017).

[35] Bruce Upbin, *IBM's Watson Gets Its First Piece of Business in Healthcare*, FORBES (February 8, 2013), https://www.forbes.com/sites/bruceupbin/2013/02/08/ibms-watson-gets-its-first-piece-of-business-in-healthcare/#48d5d2625402 (last visited June 26, 2017).

A. Finance

Many people have a mental picture of the world of finance as consisting of people in suits who make complicated investments for reasons that aren't really understood—and then proceed to take long expensive lunches and make a lot of money for it. These people are generally believed to possess a particular set of knowledge or skills that they have gained through specialized education or focused experiences that have allowed them to become familiar with the international investment market. This education and experience would appear to make them irreplaceable. However, the rise of specially designed investing programs has allowed individuals who otherwise wouldn't be considered a part of the world of finance to pierce the veil and make their own investment decisions. Considering the relatively esoteric nature of finance, the current market for those interested in financial planning has been described as presenting three options: to work with a traditional financial planner, to choose to employ "robots," or to employ "hybrids."[36]

Traditional financial planners are the people in suits—real world financial advisors. Generally these professionals are characterized by high costs that are accompanied by plenty of "hands on service."[37] The services offered by traditional financial advisors are designed for people with a lot of assets, as they frequently (but not exclusively) charge a percentage of assets under their management in exchange for their services.[38] Coincidentally this means that clients are often required to have a six-figure account to be considered. However, there are advantages to traditional financial planners, as they can provide services to their clients that robots or less specialized advisors cannot—such as assistance with risk management, legacy and estate planning, charitable giving, tax strategies, and lifestyle planning. It is also worth noting, nevertheless, that traditional financial advising firms can apply, and have been applying, AI to supplement the services they provide.[39]

---

[36] Jane Hodges, *Brains, Bots or Both? Which Financial Advisor?*, WALL ST. J. (January 6, 2015, 6:48 AM), https://www.wsj.com/articles/how-to-find-a-financial-adviser-1420516873 (last visited June 26, 2017).

[37] *Id.*

[38] *Id.*

[39] *Id.*

Across the proverbial table from traditional financial advisors you have robots, where the mantra has been "low cost but you're on your own."[40] Robots have an advantage over the traditional financial advisor when it comes to catering to those who are just starting out in financial planning. These people either are, or perceive themselves to be, unappealing to traditional financial advisors, because they generally lack substantial investments, which could mean a lesser pay out for a traditional advisor.[41] Robots cost far less than traditional advisors and work by asking customers to provide a range of information, which is then used to come up with the best portfolio to fit their needs.[42] These robot investors have been met with great success and widespread adoption; in 2016 robot advisors were estimated to have managed $60 billion in assets.[43] The same research firm which provided us with that figure believes that by 2021 robot advisors will manage nearly $385 billion in assets.[44]

Despite these figures, robotic advisors are unlikely to ever completely remove the traditional financial advisor. Traditional financial advisors at Merrill Lynch alone manage more than $2.1 trillion in assets as of 2016.[45] Robots have been a great asset for people who are just starting out with financial planning, but they are known to "offer portfolio recommendations" and in their current state are not suited for the development of big picture financial strategies.[46] Furthermore, robots are unable to provide the same level of confidence or assurances that can be found with a traditional financial advisor during rough patches.

Both traditional advisors and robots have advantages and shortcomings, so it would follow that the best choice for a financial advisor is one which brings the best of both worlds: hybrids. Robot advisors have opened the doors of financial planning to a greater population of investors

---

[40] *Id.*

[41] *Id.*

[42] *Id.*

[43] Tom Anderson, *Man vs. Machine: How to figure out if you should use a robo-advisor,* CNBC (March 13, 2017, 11:52 AM), http://www.cnbc.com/2017/03/13/man-vs-machine-how-to-figure-out-if-you-should-use-a-robo-advisor.html (last visited June 26, 2017).

[44] *Id.*

[45] *Id.*

[46] Hodges, *supra* note 36.

than in the past, but people still want someone to talk to when the market is being "bearish."[47] This idea has support from a survey conducted by Capital One Investing, which found that 74% of investors prefer to engage with an advisor during a period where markets are volatile.[48] Many traditional firms have begun providing options for hybrid services with less human involvement, but for a slimmer price.[49] Some firms that started out as providing purely robot services have also begun to take on financial advisors to provide some of the services that are lacking with the robotic approach.[50] However, some of these companies that provide robot advisors have announced that they have no intention of bringing on a human element.[51] For example, Wealthfront has stated it has no plans of providing human services to its users.[52] Andy Rachleff, Wealthfront's CEO, supported this move by saying that "young people would prefer to deal with software rather than people."[53]

Rachleff might be onto something, as there has been a growth in general distrust of financial planners since the Bernie Madoff scandal.[54] The "rise of robo-advisor" could be related to the general misunderstanding of the financial services industry, but the mistrust of flesh and blood advisors can be directly attributed to Bernie Madoff's Ponzi scheme, as that scandal revealed just how dangerous an investor could be.[55] The Ponzi scheme perpetrated by Madoff cost investors $17.5 billion and caused massive individual impact, as the life savings of many of his victims simply disappeared.[56] As of February 1, 2016, $11.079 billion of the stolen funds had been recovered, but the reputation of the finance

---

[47] *Id.*

[48] Anderson, *supra* note 43.

[49] *Id.*

[50] *Id.*

[51] *Id.*

[52] *Id.*

[53] *Id.*

[54] Richard Paxton, *Bots killing off financial advisors?,* MEDIUM (August 4, 2016), https://medium.com/@alacergroup/bots-killing-off-financial-advisors-505a399a3225 #.u09g3dv9o (last visited June 26, 2017).

[55] *Id.*

[56] *The Madoff Affair: Con of the Century,* THE ECONOMIST (December 18, 2008), http://www.economist.com/node/12818310 (last visited June 26, 2017).

industry remains tarnished.[57] Investors, especially first-time investors, would not want to work with someone they couldn't trust.[58] With that in mind, what's more trustworthy than a machine? It doesn't have any skin in the game, and will not lie to you; it only gives you the facts and what it has calculated to be the best course of action.

To answer the question of whether a financial advisor is in danger of losing his or her job to automation: it appears to be incredibly unlikely within the next twenty years. However, young professionals that are eager to break into a career in finance may find that there are fewer opportunities. It has been established that it is hard to find a substitute for the advantages that experienced financial advisors can bring to the field—especially when you consider the fact that all of that experience can be paired up with an AI to exponentially increase a financial advisor's effectiveness. You would be combining all of the efficiency of trend recognition and portfolio creation with the human touch that is desired by a significant number of investors.[59]

B. Medicine

Medicine, like law, is also considered one of the professions that is largely "immune" to automation, but artificial intelligence is in fact being experimented with to assist doctors with diagnosis. IBM's Watson has been used in an e-discovery position through the use of medical imagery databases.[60] Watson compares massive amounts of x-ray images within these databases against those of current patients and has had great success in diagnosis through comparison.[61] After the doctor is comforta-

---

[57] CNN Library, *Bernie Madoff Fast Facts*, CNN (updated May 8, 2017, 10:25 AM), http://www.cnn.com/2013/03/11/us/bernard-madoff-fast-facts/ (last visited June 26, 2017).

[58] Jordan Maglich, *Madoff Ponzi Scheme, Five Years Later*, FORBES (December 9, 2013, 10:30 AM), https://www.forbes.com/sites/jordanmaglich/2013/12/09/madoff-ponzi-scheme-five-years-later/#60616661b76a (last visited June 26, 2017).

[59] *Can Robo Advisers Replace Human Financial Advisers?*, WALL ST. J. (February 28, 2016, 10:12 PM), https://www.wsj.com/articles/can-robo-advisers-replace-human-financial-advisers-1456715553 (last visited June 26, 2017).

[60] Ariana Eunjung Cha, *Watson's Next Feat? Taking on Cancer*, WASHINGTON POST (June 27, 2015), http://www.washingtonpost.com/sf/national/2015/06/27/watsons-next-feat-taking-on-cancer/?utm_term=.21e853d0fb51 (last visited June 26, 2017).

[61] *Id.*

ble with diagnosing the problem, Watson aids in the creation of individual treatment plans by analyzing the patient's disease and treatment histories, genetic data, scans and symptoms, and then comparing them against the medical knowledge available.[62]

It is already possible for a team of doctors to create such an individualized and detailed treatment plan, but using Watson can cut the time down by days or weeks.[63] Instead of all the time required in having to photocopy medical records, send them to the relevant physicians, have those doctors physically receive the files, review them in the requisite amount of detail, and then research medical literature in the case of complex patients—Watson could feasibly have it all available in minutes.[64] Like the aforementioned Lex Machina, the idea is to take the sum of all data currently available, create a database, and then have Watson sift through that vast quantity of data to find patterns and connections that could predict what an individual patient needs.[65]

Watson has already been used in multiple hospitals, such as Memorial Sloan Kettering in New York, but IBM announced in 2013 that Watson would be utilized in a partnership with a clinic specializing in leukemia: The University of Texas MD Anderson Cancer Center.[66] Watson was utilized within MD Anderson under the title "Oncology Expert Advisor" (OEA) until relatively recently.[67] As of February 2017, MD Anderson announced it would be searching for an alternative to Watson, but this change appears to have been due to mismanagement in efforts to use Watson to develop a marketable medical technology rather than in Watson's capabilities.[68] The end of the OEA project at MD Anderson

---

[62] *Id.*

[63] *Id.*

[64] *Id.*

[65] *Id.*; *see also* Lex Machina, *supra* note 26.

[66] Cha, *supra* note 60; *MD Anderson Taps IBM Watson to Power "Moon Shots" Mission Aimed at Ending Cancer, Starting with Leukemia,* IBM (October 18, 2013), https://www-03.ibm.com/press/us/en/pressrelease/42214.wss (last visited June 26, 2017).

[67] Matthew Herper, *MD Anderson Benches Watson In Setback for Artificial Intelligence in Medicine,* FORBES (February 19, 2017, 3:48 PM), https://www.forbes.com/sites/matthewherper/2017/02/19/md-anderson-benches-ibm-watson-in-setback-for-artificial-intelligence-in-medicine/#76165de63774 (last visited June 26, 2017).

[68] *Id.*

found Watson's recommendations were in agreement with field experts 90% of the time, and Watson has appeared to have performed admirably within Memorial Sloan Kettering.[69]

Objectively, Watson is helping medical professionals select treatment plans in a streamlined manner, through efficient analysis of patient data that is already available to doctors. If AIs continue to develop in a useful fashion within the medical field, they have the potential of improving the lives of doctors and patients in a significant manner, allowing even the most rural doctors access to treatment data collected in the most advanced of cities. However, this assumes that this technology would eventually be widespread, and at the moment it is noticeably limited.

To answer the question of whether a doctor has any fear of being replaced by an AI, this also appears to be unlikely. Watson's medical application is designed to supplement the resources available to doctors, not replace them. Watson does a terrific job doing what it is designed to do, but at the moment Watson cannot interact with patients on an individual level. Although Watson can feasibly develop a treatment plan, it needs to know what it is being asked to treat.[70] In other words it requires a doctor to ask the right questions. Furthermore, even if Watson was designed to be accessible to users without a medical degree it still couldn't replace a doctor because "it lacks instinct and empathy."[71] Iltifat Husain, of Wake Forest School of medicine, has pointed out that "there are a lot of things you can deduce by what a patient is not telling you, how they interact with their families, their mood, their mannerisms. They don't look at the patient as a whole ... this is where algorithms fail you."[72] Professor Husain may have also been hinting at an unfortunate reality: patients lie.[73] There are many reasons that patients lie to their doctors, but the relevant point is that at this point in time, Watson would not be able to help a patient that was lying to it, so the human element is still absolutely essential in medicine.

---

[69] *Id.*

[70] Cha, *supra* note 60.

[71] *Id.*

[72] *Id.*

[73] Kelly K. Schwartz, *When Patients Lie to You,* Roswell Park Cancer Institute, https://www.roswellpark.org/partners-practice/white-papers/when-patients-lie-you (last visited June 26, 2017).

V. Why Is This Significant?

The widespread incorporation of AI in finance, and what could be the beginning of integration of AI into a fundamental part of medical practice, could foreshadow the future application of AI in law. The impact of AI in finance and the business models it has produced could be an indication of how the structure of law firms will change in the future. The role of AI in medicine indicates that fundamental parts of legal practice could be streamlined by the application of AI as a supplement to practice, if that's not what we are beginning to see already with the incorporation of ROSS.[74]

Law could learn a great deal from finance's use of AI, particularly the adoption of the practice models. The law equivalent of a "hybrid" firm is starting to show up in the market and there are "tech-law firms" that are trying different ways of applying technology to the practice of law.[75] The app FIXED was a prime example of how this "hybrid" approach could apply in law.[76] FIXED was an app launched in San Francisco that was similar to DoNotPay in almost every way except that the AI appeals portion was paired with one of a few local area attorneys and did not file the appeal itself.[77] Unfortunately the app eventually ran afoul of the local bar and fell out of the spotlight.[78] Local attorneys had complained about FIXED by alleging that the app was practicing law without a license, but this issue was remedied when FIXED was bought out by Lawgix, which is described as "a multi-state law firm that's actually part tech company."[79] The example still holds true, however, as Lawgix itself can serve as one of the first "hybrids" of law, combining AI and human services.

It is also worth considering that law may not be so different from finance in terms of why people want automation. There is a popular wave

---

[74] *See* Lateral Link, *supra* note 29.

[75] Sarah Perez, *Fixed, the app that helps you fight tickets, gets acquired by a law firm,* TECH CRUNCH (June 15, 2016), https://techcrunch.com/2016/06/15/fixed-the-app-that-helps-you-fight-tickets-gets-acquired-by-a-law-firm/ (last visited June 26, 2017).

[76] Josh Constine, *Hate Parking Tickets? Fixed Fights Them in Court for You,* TECH CRUNCH (January 15, 2014), https://techcrunch.com/2014/01/15/fight-parking-ticket-fixed/ (last visited June 26, 2017).

[77] *Id.*

[78] Perez, *supra* note 75.

[79] *Id.*

of support for the automation of law due to the general mistrust of attorneys from those outside of the legal field.[80] Legions of lawyers billing hundreds of dollars an hour just to tell you that you don't have a case is a popular demonization that leaves legal representation perceivably out of reach.[81] If there were AI that could make law as accessible to the layperson as it has made finance, I imagine there would be a great deal of interest in its development.

The way that AI is being implemented in medicine is very similar to law as both fields are using e-discovery to sift through large amounts of data to look for conclusions.[82] Both medicine and law could see a serious amount of time gained from the use of AI which could be put towards treating new patients or working on cases for other clients. Depending on where you stand it is also fortunate or unfortunate that law also runs into the same problems that medicine does: clients can lie. An AI in its current form would never be able to make a case without a human attorney working with the client as well. The AI would not be able to know when the client was omitting facts or know when to counsel the client as to what could happen if they didn't reveal the whole story. When it comes to managing a case, an AI wouldn't have the insight to determine an appropriate time to settle based on the other parties. It could be argued that an AI may be able to determine what the most likely settlement would be based on how parties had settled in the past, but wouldn't know when was appropriate to make an offer. Like medicine, the practice of law just requires a greater degree of human touch.

VI. Future Impacts in the Legal Field

Young attorneys in the not too distant future may be concerned about the possibility of losing work to AI. Although the kind of streamlining broad-scale that adoption of AI could lead to should be lauded, younger attorneys looking to break into the field could find their opportunities begin to shrink. The kind of work that AI is already capable of doing is

---

[80] *See* Staci Zaretsky, *Scientific Study Concludes No One Trusts Lawyers,* ABOVE THE LAW (September 24, 2014, 11:44 AM), http://abovethelaw.com/2014/09/scientific-study-concludes-no-one-trusts-lawyers/ (last visited June 26, 2017).

[81] Manjoo, *supra* note 11.

[82] *See* Complete Discovery Source, *supra* note 19.

generally the kind assigned to a legal assistant or a new lawyer.[83] The automation of this kind of entry-level work would be great for the firm as a whole or for smaller offices, but it means that fewer people would have to be employed by the firm.

Firms may also be concerned about their profits, because faster work also means that billable hours could be lost due to increased efficiency. On the other hand, reducing the amount of time that research or document review requires could be beneficial, as firms can place a greater focus on problem solving, argument drafting, and client relations rather than the mundane roles such as drafting or legal research.[84] This could also lead to the unintended result of increasing the general availability of legal services, or rather that more justiciable issues could be heard by firms. By this I mean that individuals who refrain from bringing legal action for fear of being unable to afford legal representation could find new champions in the form of AI-assisted lawyers who could potentially take on more clients because the time commitments are lower per client. This potential outcome could parallel finance, in that robot advisers made basic financial services accessible to individuals that didn't have the requisite minimums for large-scale financial planning.[85] However, this could also have consequences if AI increases issues going to court rather than being settled. It's possible that AI could also find a way to relieve the legal log jam that has backed up litigation in many courts, but how the application of AI could speed up the time it takes for a court to hear the claim is presently unclear.

What is clear is that despite the big changes that AI may bring, large firms will not feel the initial impact.[86] Like finance, the human services offered by big law give serious advantages in fields that AI just can't fill, so the rise of the Skynet law firm is a long ways away. Even so, the possible long-term impacts on the big law business are interesting to consider. The current business model for large law firms is a complicated instrument,

---

[83] Lateral Link, *supra* note 29.

[84] *Id.*

[85] Hodges, *supra* note 36.

[86] Lateral Link, *supra* note 29.

but it can be analyzed through the concepts of profit, human capital, and labor.[87]

Human capital refers to the idea that lawyers have accumulated intangible "human assets" such as legal education, experience-dependent skills, professional reputation, and relationships with clients.[88] If we conceptualize the term "labor" as the amount of time that an individual can spend earning a profit [per day], then a lawyer is limited by the amount of working hours in a day.[89] Simply put, when an attorney works (labors) he uses his human capital to make a profit. The formation of firms can be explained by the idea that experienced attorneys have more human capital than they can use in a day of labor.[90] So an experienced attorney can enter into a business relationship with a less-experienced attorney, and use some of their surplus human capital and apply it to the labor offered by a junior associate, and then maximize their profit potential.[91] In lay terms, an experienced attorney can get more work than they can possibly do, so they can get a younger attorney to assist and thereby maximize the money the firm earns. The partnership works because the junior associate gets the benefit of the experienced attorney's experience, and the senior attorney gets the associate's labor. Generally there is an uneven distribution of the profits, with the senior receiving a larger amount and the junior receiving just enough so that they are making more than they could alone, which incentivizes them to stay with the arrangement. This relationship can grow to incorporate more junior or senior attorneys to create a ratio in which the only limiting factor is the available profits; for example, one senior attorney could have enough human capital for three junior associates.

Large firms operate on the same concept, but on a much larger scale. Based on this model, AI could remove the need for junior associates. If an AI could do the same amount of labor as a junior associate, or even do more because it is able to do simple jobs faster, then the senior attorney

---

[87] Marc Galanter & Thomas M Palay, *Why the Big Get Bigger: The Promotion to Partner Tournaments and the Growth of Large Law Firms*, in LAWYERS: A CRITICAL READER 59 (Richard L. Abel, ed., 1997).

[88] *Id.*

[89] *Id.*

[90] *Id.*

[91] *Id.*

loses their incentive for entering into an arrangement with the junior attorney. This is further reinforced by the fact that the senior attorney wouldn't have to share profits with an AI. While this is a rudimentary explanation of the concept, and there are additional factors such as a younger attorney's general level of fluency with technology as compared to a senior attorney, it could turn the reasoning behind the business relationship on its head.

Still, law has been traditionally slow to adopt change. I imagine that the legal world today looks a lot like it did before the introduction of computers, or the legal databases offered by WestLaw or Lexis. There is an article from the *Arizona Attorney* published in 1994 entitled "What's all the fuss about automation?"[92] which is surprisingly similar to some of the articles I read concerning AI. This 1994 article talks about how computers can reduce the need for additional staff, and make the office far more efficient, reducing hours for billing and the need for an accounting person to keep track of all those hours.[93] Shockingly, as late as 2003 an article entitled "The 21st Century Law Office—Going Electronic Two Years Later," published in *Probate and Property*, encouraged firms to adopt fax machines for the whole office.[94] The article also encouraged firms to adopt the "paperless office" model, and to phase out their physical libraries.[95] Law offices were encouraged to modernize and incorporate scanners to reduce the need for paying such staggering amounts for off-site storage of documents.[96] I find it funny that these changes, which seem incredibly long overdue by 2003, were eliciting allusions to "cold, futuristic environments that are paperless, robotic, and hyper efficient."[97] I wonder when the day will come when law firms that don't employ AI are viewed to be as humorously out of date as a law firm without a scanner in 2003.

---

[92] Sher Hurlburt, *What's all the fuss about automation?*, ARIZ. ATTORNEY, May 1994, 21, 21.

[93] *Id.*

[94] Thomas C. Baird, *The 21st Century Law Office—Going Electronic Two Years Later*, PROB. & PROP., July-Aug. 2003, 59, 61.

[95] *Id.*

[96] *Id.*

[97] *Id.*

It is possible that lawyers and law students are standing on the precipice of the new normal in legal research. When I ask older attorneys what it was like when they went to law school, many note that "back in their day" they had to physically sift through books to do research. I will be the first to admit that I have no idea how to do legal research without a computer, so the idea that research was done with just books is impressive. Meanwhile today we consider sifting through thousands of organized sources on WestLaw or Lexis to be a draining process, even though it is much faster and much less physically involved. I can't currently imagine what law school will look like when its students have access to AI. They may remark at how daunting crafting your own searches in WestLaw would appear, instead of having ROSS do it for them, or whatever iteration of Lex Machina will be available for Lexis. It is fascinating to be witnessing the first steps of a technology that could change so much, and be adopted across so many fields, in such a short time.

VII. Conclusion

Today AI is being utilized across the country by financial planners, doctors, and now lawyers, and AIs are completing tasks in a way that could be considered the product of science fiction. But, after reviewing how they are being designed and utilized in the working world, it still appears unlikely that AI will replace the need for flesh and blood lawyers anytime soon. AIs could be a game changer in the way that research is completed or how documents are reviewed and drafted, but in their current state they are far better suited to a support role than practicing independently from a human.

qp

Visit us at *www.quidprobooks.com*.

www.ingramcontent.com/pod-product-compliance
Lightning Source LLC
Chambersburg PA
CBHW032330210326
41518CB00041B/2001